Naked Man Running

*100 IDEAS that work
in a small church*

Dave Jacobs

Copyright © 2017 Dave Jacobs
All rights reserved.

ISBN: 1976178908
ISBN 13: 9781976178900

DEDICATION

This book is dedicated to the many pastors I've had
the privilege of knowing and coaching since 2006.
Your faith and willingness to sacrifice for the sake of
your calling always amazes and encourages me. You
are not alone. You are not insignificant. Your work,
regardless of the size of your church, is of infinite value.
You are part of the majority, a noble breed called
"Small Church Pastor." I dedicate this book to you.

CONTENTS

FOREWORD BY JEFF KEADY

In January of 2013 Jonny Craig and I, almost on a whim, launched the 200churches Podcast and 200churches. com with a clear mission to provide ministry encouragement to pastors of small churches and ordinary sized churches. It wasn't long before SmallChurchPastor. com and Dave Jacobs popped up on our radar!

We invited Dave to help us produce one episode to encourage small church pastors, and that one turned into more than twenty! Friendly, spiritual, insightful, encouraging, affirming, thoughtful, challenging, and caring are words that come to mind when I think of Dave.

In the summer of 2015 my father was dying, and our family was in crisis trying to care for him. My ministry was taxing, our adult kids were marrying and moving, and our 200churches ministry was demanding. I sat in the parking lot of a Harris Teeter store in Virginia and called Dave.

I remember the words coming out of my mouth, "Dave, I feel like starting my car and driving – and not stopping, and never coming back. Is that wrong?" I knew Dave could handle my crazy, my frustration, and my verbal unload. Forty minutes later we hung up, I was a bit more psychologically and spiritually oriented, and I would survive.

When Dave writes a book about 100 ideas that work in a small church, I read it. We should all read it. These are not theoretical – they are borne out of his own pastoral ministry, as well as input from small church pastors far and wide. In fact, whatever Dave writes is borne out of his love for pastors, and his commitment to add value to them and their ministries.

My prayer is that real people will experience real blessing, because you, pastor, implement some of these ideas! Enjoy.

Jeff Keady is the co-founder of 200churches.com, a blog and weekly audio podcast designed to encourage and inspire pastors of smaller churches. Along with his partner Jonny Craig, they have created a unique place to share ideas, ask questions, and build relationships with others who minister in similar settings.

PREFACE

Did you know when people exclaim "*Eureka!*" they are reenacting a legendary event in the life of the Greek mathematician and inventor Archimedes? (287 BC - 212 BC) While wrestling with the problem of how to determine the purity of gold, he made the sudden realization that the buoyancy of an object placed in water is equal in magnitude to the weight of the water the object displaces. According to one popular version of the legend, he made his discovery at a public bath-house, whereupon he leapt out of his bath, exclaimed "*Eureka! Eureka!*" ("I have found it!"), and ran home naked through the streets. (Source: Merriam-Webster. com) Hence the name of this book, Naked Man Running: 100 IDEAS that work in a small church.

For the past ten years I have been coaching pastors of smaller churches. These leaders are always searching for answers and ideas that will relate to the unique challenges of pastoring a small church. Often times frustrated, they return from conferences led by pastors of larger churches either telling them how to grow their church or offering them ideas that simply won't work in a small church.

A few years ago I realized that I had been accumulating "eureka-moments," ideas and solutions for the everyday problems pastors face. Some of these were written down and others tucked away in the back of my head. I thought up some of these "How-to's," and many of them came about while thinking and brainstorming with other small church pastors. A light went on. "Eureka!" I didn't jump up from my bathtub and go running down the street naked, but I did think, "Why not gather all these ideas in one volume and categorize them into something that resembled a reference book that pastors could easily turn to for solutions to their specific problems?"

Much to my surprise I discovered that I had one hundred and thirty four ideas! Some of them were not as good as others. So, deciding that one hundred was a good round number, I set about to narrow things down to only the best.

Originally I was going to simply call this book, "100 IDEAS that work in a small church." Then I thought of naming it "Eureka," or "Eureka-Moment." When I researched the origins of the word "eureka" I discovered this naked man running by the name of Archimedes. "Eureka!" I found the perfect name for this book.

"Naked Man Running: 100 IDEAS that work in a small church" is the result of ten years of coaching. I guess you can read it from beginning to end as you would any book, but you might find it helpful to look over the table of contents and pick out one or two ideas that relate to your current situation. Many of these ideas include questions for reflection that you can use with your leaders. Once again, think of it as a reference book, a manual filled with "Eureka-Moments." But remember, when you find that perfect idea, don't go running down the street naked or you might end up in jail. I don't have a chapter on how to get out of jail without losing your job.

PASTORAL SKILLS

1

HOW TO STOP DOING PREMARITAL COUNSELING

Most couples that go to premarital counseling sit there madly in love, starry-eyed, moving their heads up and down in agreement to anything and everything the pastor tells them. The problem is that being married is a theory to them, there's no hands-on experience. They don't know what they don't know. I now ask pastors to consider abandoning the traditional approach to premarital counseling for post-marital counseling.

Instead of meeting with a couple five to seven weeks in a row to talk about communication, money, in-laws, sex, the different love languages, etc., meet twice before they get married. The first meeting can be your chance to get to know them and to make sure there not about the make the biggest mistake in their lives. The second meeting can be to plan the ceremony. Then, after they're married, meet once at the three-month mark, once at the six-month mark, once at the nine-month mark and once at their one-year anniversary.

Believe me, when they meet with you after having some experience being married they will have a long list of things they want to talk to you about. You'll be dealing with real-life situations and find yourself scratching where they itch. If you feel that you just have to give them some more input before they get married then give them a good book to read to hold them over (or to hold you over) until your first meeting scheduled three months after the wedding.

This approach to pre-marital counseling, which is really more post-marital counseling, will be easier on your schedule and more meaningful and effective to the couples you marry.

2

HOW TO BE MORE PRODUCTIVE AND MOVE YOUR PEOPLE IN THE RIGHT DIRECTION

Pastoring sometimes feels like being on a treadmill, you're exerting a lot of energy, but you're not going anywhere.

Just because you're busy does not mean that you are productive. The trick is not to work harder, but smarter. In fact, the smarter you work, the less number of hours you need to be productive. It is possible to be a better pastor in less time.

To be more productive and ensure you're moving your church in the right direction, you need to focus on 'The Three P's.'

Product: Your product is people. But not just any people, you're trying to produce followers of Jesus. Few pastors would argue with this. However, if you get a group of pastors together and ask them what a 'follower of Jesus' looks like, you will get different answers. That's okay. What's not okay is having some vague idea of what it looks like to be a follower of Jesus.

I suggest you draw up a list, don't make it too long or it will end up being unattainable, of what practices, attitudes, and focus, a follower of Jesus should have. Is it clear to you what your product is?

Preaching: Too many pastors preach without purpose. There is often no rhyme or reason to the things they decide to teach on. Whatever you are trying to produce needs to be reflected in your preaching. You preach on 'this' to produce 'that.' Are you preaching with a purpose?

Programming: Just as there needs to be a purpose to our preaching, there also needs to be a purpose to our programming. We do 'this' because we are trying to produce 'that.' Ministries or programs in your church that do not reflect or produce your 'that,' need to be evaluated and sometimes eliminated.

Is there anything your church does that is not producing your 'that'?

Do you know what your product is?

Are you preaching with a purpose?

Do your programs help produce the product you want?

This might be a great topic for discussion at your next leadership team meeting.

3

HOW TO TRAIN PEOPLE TO BE MORE FRIENDLY ON SUNDAYS

I remember once when Ellen and I were visiting a church; we decided to play the 'Friendly Game.' It's really simple, what you do is stand in the back of the meeting room and look confused. Then you keep track how many times someone says "hi" to you. Greeters don't count because that's their job. The 'Stand up and greet someone.' time doesn't really count because they've been told to do it. The pastor, or the pastor's spouse, don't count because they get paid to be friendly.

Would your church win the Friendly Game? I find it interesting how many pastors say their church is really friendly, but when someone visits their church it must have been the Sunday when all the friendly ones stayed home. At least that's what some visitors report.

There are a number of reasons why Christians aren't friendly to visitors on Sunday, for example:

1. Some are too busy talking to their friends, which is not necessarily a bad or unreasonable thing.
2. Some people are just not friendly people. They're not picking on church visitors; they're not friendly to anyone.
3. Some people are shy.
4. Some don't know what to say after, "Hi, my name is Dave."

Visitors don't expect a lot. It doesn't take much for a guest to feel like they've been warmly welcomed. Here are four simple questions that anyone, even the shy ones in your church, can ask when approaching a visitor. Challenge your people to memorize these questions:

"Hi, my name is Dave. What's your name?"

"How did you hear about our church?"

"What do you do for a living?"

"I hope you enjoy today, and I hope to see you again next week."

And if they are really brave, they can pull a friend over and introduce them to the visitor.

Train your people to do this.

If guests don't feel your church was very friendly, there is a good chance they will not return. This Sunday if you see two people in the back looking confused, it could be Ellen and me.

4

HOW TO DO INTERNSHIPS
IN A SMALL CHURCH

Back in my Bible College days, senior students had to complete an internship in a local church before they could graduate. The idea behind this was that the hands-on experience of ministering in a church would bring balance to the academic instruction in the classroom. The student saw this as an exciting opportunity to "show what they got" in a real ministry environment.

For the Pastor agreeing to take on an intern it was viewed as "cheap labor." The larger churches in the area would pay their interns (though as little as they could get away with), which made these 'paying gigs,' the first choice of those looking for an internship.

Years later, after I had left college and was pastoring, a young, talented ministry student approached me for an internship. I explained I could not pay him with anything other than direct contact with me. We set up a plan, and he seemed genuinely excited about having an opportunity to be mentored and trained. A couple of days later I got a call from him explaining that he had decided to take an internship somewhere else. When I asked him why, he admitted that another larger church pays their interns and that he would be going with them.

Sigh.

An internship is a chance for someone to receive hands-on training, mentoring, and experience, in a church setting. Small church pastors often think they can't offer internships because they are small or because they can't pay. But you can do internships without shelling out one dime. You can do internships even though you pastor a small church. You can do internships even though you don't live near a Christian College that has young ministry students. But first, answer this question: Do you have any of the following people in your church:

Older Christians who are retired and have some free time?

Christians who are currently unemployed or in-between jobs and have some free time?

Mothers with children in school who have some free time?

College-age Christians who are interested in ministry and have flexibility and free time?

I bet you have some people like this in your congregation. All of these people might be interested in doing an internship. Some will have more time on their hands and some less. Some, especially those in-between jobs, might have to stop the internship midway when they find a job. That's ok.

Internships help fulfill our mandate to make disciples, raise up leaders, and delegate ministry. In the long run, you might just be saving yourself time (by delegating some of your responsibilities to interns) and expanding your ministry without spending one penny.

5

HOW TO INCREASE
'DELEGATION-SUCCESS' BY 70%

For most pastors, the idea of delegation is not new. We've all heard sermons about Jethro, Moses' father in law, who advised Moses to release others to help him bear the load of leading God's people.

It's essential for the busy pastor to not only delegate, but also delegate well. You don't want the task you've delegated to be handed back to you later.

Here are seventeen questions to ask before you delegate that will increase 'Delegation-Success' by 70%.

1. Have I adequately prayed and asked the Holy Spirit to lead me to the right person?
2. What type of skills, giftings, and passions am I looking for in the person I choose?
3. Who can do what I do at least 70% as well as me?

4. Have I sought a second opinion from someone about delegating this task to this person?
5. When will I set up a meeting to attempt to recruit this person?
6. What information will I need to bring with me for my meeting once it's scheduled?
7. Who will be affected by this person's new task?
8. Will any of those who will be affected need to be informed ahead of time?
9. What training will be needed for this person to succeed?
10. What time commitment will need to be made to get them ready?
11. What resources will they need to carry out their responsibilities?
12. Have I communicated to them that this will be on a trial basis with a review after an agreed upon period of time? (If it's not working for them, or for you, then they can get out gracefully.)
13. Have I built an off-ramp? An off-ramp provides a way out. (see question 12)

Side Note: We need to provide training as to how one resigns from a ministry responsibly.

14. How much time will I give this person to get back to me with an answer?

15. Do I have a second choice in case this person decides against taking on this task?
16. If the person says yes, how much time will this free up for me?
17. Do I have a prioritized list of remaining action steps I will need to take?

6

HOW TO BUILD A SUSTAINABLE LEADERSHIP BASE

I want to share with you the five steps needed for a sustainable leadership base. In other words, how can I get leaders, keep leaders, and get more leaders? The answer to this is found in these five words: Identify, Recruit, Train, and Repeat.

Identify: Identify those with leadership potential. When looking for leaders remember what I call the "4 C's":

> Character: Do they demonstrate Christian maturity?
>
> Competency: Do they have the skills or gifts necessary for their task?
>
> Chemistry: Do the two of you get along well with each other?
>
> Commitment: Are they committed to the vision and direction of your church?

Recruit: Whenever recruiting someone, remember these three things: 1) be very clear about your expectations, 2) have a written ministry job description, 3) let the person know this will be an experiment, on a trial basis.

People are much more likely to say yes when they know they have a way out if they end up not liking their ministry. You might say, "Let's try this for a few months and see how it works out. If you end up feeling like this ministry is a bad fit for you then we will find you a replacement. And in the event that I come to the conclusion that this ministry is a bad fit for you, will you give me permission to tell you and to try and find a different area of service more fitting for your gifts and skill-set?"

Train: Different ministries require different training. Someone leading a small group needs a different skill-set than someone who helps out in children's ministry. Ask yourself what specific training will this person need in order to succeed?

Maintain: Just because you've identified a leader, successfully recruited them, and adequately trained them, does not mean your job is over. Leaders need to be maintained. What will your plan be to provide ongoing encouragement and resourcing? Remember the rule: If you don't maintain your leaders, they will not stay your leaders.

Repeat: Recruiting never ends. You can never have too many leaders. You never know when someone is going to move out of town or get mad and leave the church. Leaders are always looking for leaders.

If you want a sustainable leadership base in your church, you must identify, recruit, maintain, and repeat.

7

HOW TO GET ORGANIZED
AND STAY ORGANIZED

Over the years, I've gathered some simple tools that keep my busy life, business, and ministry, flowing smoothly.

It's not uncommon for me to run across pastors who are, basically, disorganized. They miss appointments, let important things slip through the cracks, and are often overwhelmed by what seems to be a life out of control.

The first step in getting your life in control, rather than out of control, organized versus disorganized, is to gather some simple organizational tools. Here's my list:

1. You need a calendar, preferably one that you can sync with your home computer, work computer, and phone. I know this sounds

elementary, but it's not unusual for me to run across a pastor who tries to keep everything clear in their mind rather than in a calendar.

2. Set **phone alarms.** Most phones allow you to set alarms to go off reminding you of events and appointments. I have alarms that go off on my phone five minutes before every coaching call I'm scheduled to make that day. This is another way to ensure that I don't get caught up in some project and forget an appointment.

3. You need to have **a 'notes' notebook.** Instead of scribbling thoughts and notes on scraps of paper that pile up all over your desk, put all of those bits of random information in one notebook. More on this in a minute.

4. **Post-it Notes.** One of the greatest inventions of man, from a standpoint of developing organizational skills, is the Post-it Note. But the Post-it Note must be posted someplace where you're guaranteed to see it. Like on your computer monitor, bathroom mirror, door to your office, etc.

5. Each day **look ahead** to see what's coming the following day. One of the final things I do at the end of my workday is to make sure I'm aware of and prepared for tomorrow.

6. **To do list.** Once again, I know this sounds elementary, but the old tried-and-true 'To do list' has long been a staple of those who are organized.

I want to explain in greater detail the 'notes' notebook.

First, you need to get two notebooks. The first notebook needs to be thought of as a 'junk drawer.' You probably have one of these in your home. We have one. Ours is filled with little odds and ends, no rhyme or reason, just things we toss in there thinking that one day we may need them. I love going through my junk drawer; it's like a treasure chest, I never know what I'll find in there.

Instead of jotting down phone numbers, things to remember, the name of that book your friend mentioned over the phone, on separate pieces of paper that end up strewn all over your desk, everything like this goes into one notebook. No more random slips of paper. Everything you jot down can be easily retrieved in one place. Never again will you ask, "Now where did I put that piece of paper?"

Next, you need to get a second notebook. This is not a junk drawer. This is the one place where you keep all of your ideas. My 'ideas' notebook is divided into different categories: ministry products I'm thinking of developing, article ideas for my blog and website, book projects, sermon ideas, etc. This isn't a junk drawer notebook, but an 'ideas' notebook. I have found this to be so helpful. When it's time for me to write a new blog post, or begin working on a sermon, all I need do is bring out my notebook, and a list of ideas are waiting for me.

If you want to get organized and stay organized one of the best tools is the 'notes' notebook.

I want to give you five easy steps to get and stay organized:

1. Brainstorm and come up with a list of everything in your personal life and ministry life that needs organizing.
2. Prioritize that list.
3. Ask yourself, "Are there any tools that I need to get organized?"
4. Assign dates and times to begin to work on the things on your list.
5. In three months evaluate how well your organization plan is working and make any adjustments as needed.

Getting and staying organized is not difficult, but it does require certain tools and a specific plan to ensure that we stay on top of the things that we need to stay on top of.

8

HOW TO MAKE A GREAT DECISION IN FIVE EASY STEPS

Pastors are always making decisions. Some decisions are minor, "Should we offer donuts or bagels or both on Sunday mornings?" Some decisions are major, "Should I ask Bob to become a board member?" Whether the issue is big or small, minor or major, pastors are faced with decisions. Learning how to make great decisions is a skill. I've discovered five essentials for making great decisions.

1. Great decisions are preceded by great thinking. Leadership guru John Maxwell believes that the hardest thing to get people to do is, "...to think, and to do things in order of importance." My experience in working with leaders would cause me to agree. Thinking must precede decisions.

2. Thinking needs to be thought of as a spiritual discipline. For me, thinking is not simply some mental exercise, but a spiritual exercise. When we sit down to think, we need to invite the Holy Spirit to come and help us think.

3. Time must be set apart for thinking. Usually, we do our thinking on the run or in the midst of distraction. This is not an entirely useless way to think, but it will not result in the best thinking. We need to set apart specific time for the sole purpose of thinking. Think-time should be scheduled into our week and show up in our calendar like any other appointment.

4. We must make sure we are thinking about what we should be thinking about. This is where the Holy Spirit comes in. We set apart thinking time, but we don't rush into it. We pause, we wait, we pray, "Holy Spirit, I think I know what I need to think about, but I wait upon You. Show me what I need to be thinking about." This cautious and reflective approach will often lead us into areas of thinking we might not have anticipated.

5. When thinking, be begin by asking the right questions, rather than looking for the right answers. Questions always result in answers. Great questions get great answers. No questions get no answers. For example, if I am faced with the decision whether or not to ask Bob to become

a board member. I need to think through questions such as:

1) What am I looking for in a board member?
2) How did I come up with these criteria?
3) Why do I feel Bob is a good fit?

These are great questions that will result in a great decision.

Let me challenge you to write into your calendar think-time. Find a place relatively free from distraction. Bring along a yellow-pad or whatever you use to jot down notes and ideas. Sit down and pray; invite the Holy Spirit to invade your thinking. Ask questions; write down the answers that come to you.

If you follow these five simple essentials, you'll find yourself making great decisions.

9

HOW TO IDENTIFY A LEADER
IN THREE EASY STEPS

eadership Rule: It's easier to get them in, than it is to get them out.

When selecting leaders look for: Character, Competence, and Ownership.

Look for character.

African-American educator Booker T. Washington (1856-1915) said, "Character is power." The person with character has power...power to lead. People will follow a man or woman with character. Character isn't developed overnight. You will need time and contact with the person to recognize whether or not they have character. Don't rush to put someone into a key position of leadership until you've spotted signs of character.

What do they talk about, laugh about, value?

How do they spend their free time, treat their spouse, or talk to those under them?

Are they reliable, punctual, courteous, and kind?

Are they impatient, critical, or condescending?

How do they handle disagreement, personal criticism, and conflict?

It takes time to recognize character. Be patient. Here's the rule: The more important the position of leadership, the longer you should take in making your decision.

Look for competence.

Competency is the ability to do something well or to a required standard. Some pastors set their leadership standards too high and others too low. Both extremes will prevent a church from moving forward. If you're thinking of making someone your new worship leader, you want a certain level of competence. Someone leading a small group needs some competency in speaking, facilitating, etc. The church bookkeeper needs to be good with numbers. Now remember, some skills can be learned, and this might mean you will need to invest the time to equip them, but in the long run, it will be worth the initial investment. It would be better to leave a ministry spot empty and wait for a competent person to fill it, than to assign to it someone who will end up causing you a headache because of their incompetence.

Look for ownership.

It's hard to keep someone motivated in a ministry if they do not have ownership. That's why you've got to be careful about talking someone into doing something they really don't want to do. They might say "yes", but you don't want to be pushing and pulling them all the time. People who have ownership of a ministry will be self-motivated.

Ownership, character, and competence are three essential qualities to look for before setting apart someone in a key position of leadership. Save yourself a headache, select leaders slowly and carefully. Remember the rule: It's easier to get them in, than it is to get them out.

10

HOW TO HAVE PRODUCTIVE
AND MEANINGFUL MEETINGS

If, somehow in your training, you missed that class on Meaningful Meetings, you're probably sunk. Why do I say this? Because pastors are always calling meetings.

We have board meetings, deacon meetings, leadership team meetings, Elders meetings, meetings to train, and planning meetings. Some churches have meetings to plan future meetings.

One essential skill for the small church pastor is to know how to have meaningful and productive, "This was really worth my time" meetings. I think the pastor who has a meaningless, unproductive, boring meeting should have to spend a night in the county jail. Here are my twelve ways to insure meaningful and productive meetings.

1. <u>Have an agenda</u>. Write the agenda down. Don't rely on your memory. Don't go to the meeting unprepared and call it "being led by the Spirit."

2. <u>Have a limited agenda</u>. Too many things to cover in one night will reduce the meaningfulness and productivity of the meeting.

3. <u>Have a prioritized agenda</u>. Some things on your agenda are probably not as important as other things. First things first, second things second.

4. <u>Always distribute your agenda ahead of time.</u> Team members need to know what the focus will be, and have time to think about the agenda before the meeting.

5. <u>Stick to the agenda</u>.

6. <u>Agree upon a time limit for each person to share</u>. Often the reason why our meetings are not as meaningful and productive as they could be is that someone talked too long. If you have some 'talkers' in your group, a three-minute egg timer works really well. I'm serious.

7. <u>Only have a meeting when you truly need to have a meeting</u>. One leader I recently spoke to had a once a month leadership team meeting until he discovered that they didn't need to meet that often. He cut back to every other month and guess what? Nobody complained.

8. <u>Never allow a meeting to run late into the night</u>, especially on a weeknight when people

have to get up early the next day for work. The later you go the more tired they are, and the more tired they are, the less meaningful and productive the meeting will be.

9. Individuals who sabotage meetings must be spoken to. Don't allow someone to dominate or take the group off the agenda.

10. Facilitate don't dominate. Pastors tend to talk too much at meetings.

11. There should be at least two leadership meetings per year that are fun-focused rather than ministry or business-focused. All work and no play makes, not only Tom a dull boy, but a dull leadership team. Do something fun together.

12. Teach 'meeting etiquette.' To have productive and meaningful leadership team meetings, you might need to train your leaders how to have a productive and meaningful leadership team meeting. By 'meeting etiquette' I mean rules such as:

I will not dominate.
I will treat others with honor and respect.
I will not interrupt.
I will participate.
I will not lead the group down a rabbit-trail.

11

HOW TO DEVELOP A MISSION STATEMENT THAT IS NOT A WASTE OF TIME

A long with an obsession with church growth and numbers, we can thank the Church Growth Movement of the 80's and 90's for introducing to us the importance of "Mission Statements."

Mission statements can be a waste of time, and mission statements can be worth your time. But first, allow me to make a few observations concerning mission statements.

1. These days, almost every church has a mission statement. However, this is a relatively new phenomenon.
2. I am always amazed at the amount of time pastors and their boards will invest in coming up with a mission statement. One pastor told me

that he and his board had just completed a three-month project developing their mission statement.

3. Despite attempts to come up with something new and catchy, most mission statements basically sound the same.

I'm not suggesting that we throw out our mission statements or, if we currently don't have one, that we don't bother coming up with one. All I'm suggesting is that mission statements can be a waste of time, if...

1. They serve no purpose other than providing something to put on our business cards, letterhead, or website.
2. They are way too long for anyone to commit to memory.
3. The words chosen are confusing to normal people and thus require a constant explanation as to what our mission statement means.

On the other hand, mission statements are worth our time, if...

1. They remind us what we are in business for, or what's important to us.
2. They help remind the people of our church what we are in business for or what's important to us.

So, if you have a mission statement, are coming up with your very first mission statement, or are revisiting or revamping your current mission statement, keep in mind:

1. Keep it as short and sweet and clear as possible. Make it something easy to remember.
2. Revisit your mission statement often. Let it be the guiding light by which you program, plan, and preach. Your mission statement lets you know who you are and who you're not. Knowing who you're not, can be as important as knowing who you are.

12

HOW TO KNOW IF YOU ARE WORKING TOO MANY HOURS

Does your workweek work? By the weekend do you feel weakened?

In my coaching practice, I regularly make two observations:

1) The average pastor's calendar is too full.
2) Often the tasks that make up the pastors work-week do not reinforce the vision the pastor has for the church. As a result, the pastor ends up spending much of their time doing almost everything other than pastoring and moving the church towards their goals.

To have a workweek that works, a workweek that won't make you weak, you must ask yourself three questions:

1) Are the number of hours I'm working for the church sustainable? I don't believe that forty-five to fifty or more hours a week is sustainable. Eventually, somewhere down the road, something is going to break down. It might be you. It could take years, but eventually one will see the results of more than fifty hours a week, especially if one neglects their days off, vacation time, and quiet times with the Lord.

2) Are the tasks that make up my workweek effective? By effective I mean, are they moving me towards my vision for the church, or away from my vision for the church? Do the tasks that make up my workweek reinforce my call to pastor, or do they reinforce other things that have little, if anything, to do with shepherding people?

3) Is my workweek pleasurable? I realize that in any job there will be some tasks that you enjoy more than others, and this is certainly true for the pastor. Not everything that makes up your workweek will be enjoyable. But if you are not doing more enjoyable things than unenjoyable things, eventually you will burn out. A great exercise for pastors is to look at the tasks that make up their workweek, and identify those things they draw energy from versus those things that drain energy from them. You must have more energy-givers then energy-drainers.

When was the last time you seriously looked at how you spend your week? Is your workweek sustainable, effective, and pleasurable?

13

HOW TO BE A BETTER PASTOR IN LESS TIME

Okay, this one is for all you old-timers out there who still remember the greatest rock band ever, The Beatles. In December of 1964, the song "Eight Days a Week" was released on their album entitled, Beatles For Sale. Paul, in 1984, credited the title of the song to Ringo Starr. However, Paul had also credited the title to an actual chauffeur who once drove him to John Lennon's house in Weybridge England. Paul said, "I usually drove myself there, but the chauffeur drove me out that day and I said, "How have you been?" He said, "All right, working hard, working eight days a week."

Have you ever felt like there were not enough hours in the day or days in the week? With all the things that keep you busy, wouldn't it be nice if there were an eighth day? One of the most common complaints I hear from pastors is, "I just don't have enough time."

I believe we have exactly enough time to do the things God has asked us to do. "Not enough time" is often an indication that we are doing things God has not asked us to do.

Our congregants will tell us what we should be doing. The schools we were trained in will tell us what we should be doing. The church we came from or were raised in will tell us what we should be doing. Conferences, books, seminars, blogs, all tell us what we should be doing. All of these can add ministry tasks to our workweek that result in a 'busyness' of life that is counterproductive to our call as a pastor and to the health of our souls.

Eugene Peterson, in his excellent book, *Five Smooth Stones For Spiritual Leadership* said, "The pastor must not be "busy." Busyness is an illness of spirit, a rush from one thing to another because there is no ballast of vocational integrity and no confidence in the primacy of grace. In order for there to be conversation and prayer that do the pastoral work of meeting the intimacy needs among people, there must be a wide margin of quiet leisure that defies the functional, technological, dehumanizing definitions that are imposed upon people (and pastors) by others in the community."

Do you find yourself wishing there were more hours in the day? Could you use an eighth day of the week? Is it possible that your feelings of, "I just don't have enough time." are the result of taking on tasks and responsibilities that did not originate from God?

Questions for reflection:

1. How might I discover those things that fill up my workweek and have their origins from places other than God?

2. What steps could I take to remove those tasks, focus more fully on the things I'm certain God has asked me to do, and therefore, free up my schedule so there is no need for more hours or more days in my week?

14

HOW TO BEAT
PROCRASTINATION...TOMORROW

You might be thinking, "One of these days I'm going to get help for my problem with procrastination." Well, today is that day.

Everyone struggles with procrastination to one degree or another. Type A personalities live like there's no tomorrow. The rest of us live like there is. In fact, Mark Twain once said, "Never put off until tomorrow what you can do the day after tomorrow."

There are four reasons why we procrastinate. Identifying and understanding these reasons are the first steps towards victory over procrastination.

Reason #1: Fatigue. I'm overweight. You know you're overweight when you can't get off the couch without making a grunting sound. On top of that, I don't get much exercise, other than getting off of the couch. Add to this that I don't sleep well, and you have a great recipe for feeling tired all the time. When I feel tired, I put things off.

Reason #2: Distractions. (Wait a minute. I'll be right back. Someone just emailed me.) There...now, where were we? Oh yes, distractions. Distractions are one reason why we put things off. Social media is a big distraction. All the interesting stuff available on the web is a big distraction. A noisy environment is distracting. People dropping in unannounced are distracting. Your phone, or the things you are worried about, can be distracting.

Reason #3: Unenjoyable. This is a big reason for procrastination. If I don't enjoy a certain task, there is a greater likelihood that I will put off doing it. For example, I don't enjoy doing the accounting for my business. Instead of staying on top of it, I'll let things pile up for a few months, start worrying about an IRS audit, and then spend a couple of hours catching up. We tend to put off those things that we don't enjoy. I've had an email from my dentist sitting in my inbox for two months reminding me to come in for a check-up.

Reason #4: Incompetence. When you're not good at something, it's easy to procrastinate. There's not a lot of things that I'm good at. I think there are about three things I'm good at and one of them is whistling. Anything involving, tools, fixing, assembling, anything requiring coordination, stuff like this, I'm not good at.

For the past three summers, I've wanted to fix a series of faulty sprinkler-heads on our property. I'm not good at fixing things. When I try to fix things I typically make the problem worse. But I swear to you today, on the souls of my grandchildren, next summer I'll fix those sprinkler-heads.

So, there they are, the four most common reasons for procrastination. Do you recognize any of them in your life? Here are some questions for reflection:

1. Which of these four relates to you the most?
2. Can you think of any other reasons why you procrastinate that are not on this list?
3. What three decisions could you make today (not tomorrow) that would help you beat procrastination?

15

HOW TO EVALUATE
YOUR CHURCH

Occasionally we need to sit down and evaluate how effective our ministry is. Paul told Archippus, "Pay attention your ministry, which has been given you by God, so that you may fulfill it." (Col. 4:17) Paul encouraged Timothy, "Take seriously your responsibilities as a pastor, be absorbed in them so that everyone will be able to see your progress." (1 Tim 4:15)

Don't be afraid to evaluate how effective the different ministries in your church are. Don't obsess, but don't neglect to examine the programs your church offers. Below you'll find my best questions to ask when evaluating ministries. You can either go through these on your own or with your key leaders.

1. What will be the measure we use to evaluate?
2. Why do we feel this is a good measure?

3. Can we identify any weaknesses with our criteria?

4. Are we including the right people in the evaluation process?

5. With our criteria in mind, on a scale of 1-10 (one being lowest), how would we rate our ministry or specific department?

6. What would need to happen to bump that number up one or two points?

7. What will our next action steps be?

Once or twice a year, set apart some good thinking time for the sole purpose of evaluating the different key ministries in your church. It's difficult to know if your church is effective without times of evaluation.

16

HOW TO WRITE A MINISTRY JOB DESCRIPTION

I read an article from a man who has a ministry of training church volunteers. Apparently, there were about one hundred such people attending a seminar from this man, and he asked a question, "How many of you here have a job description that is clear, on paper, that was given to you by either your supervisor at your church or your pastor?" Only thirty percent raised their hands.

Follow-up questions revealed that this lack of a job description created a great deal of frustration on the part of the church-worker. The article concluded that it's important to develop ministry job descriptions.

I often hear from pastors that they need to develop job descriptions. That's good. What's not so good is that this tells me they currently don't have ministry job descriptions. And if the poll of those who attended the seminar I mentioned above is any indicator of a universal reality, then there's a good chance these pastors have volunteers who are frustrated. One more thing, is it possible that some of our frustrations with leaders can be traced back to a lack of a job description? Perhaps.

Let me ask you; do those who serve in key positions of ministry in your church have a job description? Is the job description written down? If not, might I suggest you begin the process of developing ministry job descriptions for those who serve in your church? The following are four simple principles to follow.

First, job descriptions must be clear. Don't rush through the process. Have you thought through every detail? Have you written this out in a way that is understandable? Rule: Never underestimate your ability to be vague when all the while thinking you are being clear. Is it clear?

Second, job descriptions must be realistic. It doesn't matter what you want the person to do; it only matters what they have the will and the time to do. The more requirements or expectations you have, the fewer volunteers you'll be able to pick from. Be flexible. Are you asking too much? Remember, these people have lives outside of the church. Be realistic.

Third, job descriptions must contain a way to measure success. How will you and the volunteer know that they are doing a good job? What specific things are you both looking for?

Fourth, job descriptions need an off-ramp. Is there a plan to make it easy for the person to quit or for you to move them out and into another position better suited for them if need be? Circumstances change, people change, needs change. Give people a ministry, but start them out on a trial basis. Let them know that after a few months you'll meet with them to determine if they want to keep going. Tell them if it doesn't work out, they'll be able to quit. More people will be willing to commit if they know they can get out if they don't end up liking it. Also, let them know that if you end up thinking it's not working out that you would like permission to move them into something that's a better match.

Rule: It's easier to get them in, than it is to get them out. Have an off-ramp.

17

HOW TO INSURE THE VALUES OF YOUR CHURCH ARE NOT FORGOTTEN

Anything worth saying is worth pounding.

The values you hold as a church (We value worship, We value outreach, We value Bible-teaching, etc., you come up with your own list.) are important. If you want to effectively communicate your values, then you will need to repeat them over and over, and pound them into the minds of your people. Notice I said, "effectively communicate?"

Effective communication results in both comprehension and action. I can preach a sermon, but that's no guarantee my congregation will comprehend (understand) or apply (take action upon) my words. I must not assume communication is occurring just because words are flowing. Certain things enhance communication. As a pastor, you are a professional communicator. Professionals are always honing their skills. One communication skill is repetition. Repetition ensures communication.

Whatever your values are (those things you want your church to focus on), they will need to be hammered and pounded, repeated and reinforced, again and again and again. For example, if you want your people to be 'givers' it won't be enough to preach on giving once a year. We won't produce people who 'share their faith' as a result of one great sermon on personal evangelism. Repetition ensures communication.

Exercise #1. Draw up a list of your most important values. Don't make it too long.

When I was pastoring my 'values list' looked something like this:

1. I want my people to be humble.
2. I want my people to have a consistent and meaningful devotional life.
3. I want my people to be inviters and includers.
4. I want my people to be givers.
5. I want my people to be servants.
6. I want my people to be patient, and gentle, and forgiving towards one another.
7. I want my people to be suspicious of their cultures attempts to influence them.

Maybe your list will be different, maybe longer, and maybe shorter. The important thing is that you identify your values.

Next, plan your next twelve months of preaching around your values. If you tend to teach topically, then this will be easy. If you tend to focus on book studies, be on the lookout for your values coming up within the context of your book study and reinforce them when they do.

The bottom line is this: repeating your values will ensure communication, comprehension, and action.

Exercise #2. Identify ways to reinforce and repeat your values other than through your preaching and teaching ministry.

I remember communicating my values through the literature we made available, and the type of programs we implemented. In addition to this, I would talk about our values in leadership team meetings and new member classes. What ideas can you come up with?

You are trying to create a certain kind of church. This "kind of church" is based on your values. If it's important enough to be a value, then it's important enough to bear repeating. People learn through repetition. Communication is enhanced through repetition.

What values do your people need hammered into them over the next twelve months? Develop a plan and start pounding.

18

HOW TO AVOID MAKING MISTAKES WHEN PLACING SOMEONE IN LEADERSHIP

"It's easier to get them in, than it is to get them out." Repeat that three times. Get a tattoo that says, "It's easier to get them in, than it is to get them out." I don't care how you do it...never forget the rule, "It's easier to get them in, than it is to get them out." In regards to selecting leaders, it's easier to get them in, than it is to get them out.

When I was starting out as a pastor, I made my fair share of mistakes when placing someone in leadership. Have you noticed that you tend to learn more from doing things wrong than you do from doing things right? My failures taught me five ways to avoid making mistakes when placing someone in leadership.

1. Don't put someone in leadership just because they were a pastor. Now don't get me wrong; this ex-pastor might turn out to be a great help and encouragement to you, but first, find out why they are a 'former-pastor.' Call their last church and see if they left in good standing. Retired pastors are often a great addition to a church as long as they are coming with no agenda and are able to be part of the church instead of in charge of the church. This is a difficult transition for some retired or former pastors to make. All I'm saying is don't start jumping up and down because someone comes through your doors that used to be a pastor.

2. Don't put someone in leadership simply because they have a lot of Bible knowledge. Just because they can quote Leviticus or produce a verse for every situation, does not mean they are mature or have leadership potential. Bible knowledge does not guarantee character, maturity, or leadership. You can teach a parrot to quote scripture, but they seldom make good elders.

3. Don't put someone in leadership just because they have zeal. The Greek word for zeal is 'de-los', a derivative of 'deo' meaning "to boil", or to "throb with heat." Have you ever spoken to someone who was "On fire for the Lord?"

I've had people tell me that they were "On fire for the Lord." I knew what they meant, but it was hard for me not to laugh, which probably proves that I'm not "On fire for the Lord." The point is, enthusiasm, excitement, and zeal, are not necessarily the same thing as character, maturity or leadership.

4. Don't put people in leadership just because they have been a Christian for a long time. Years should produce maturity, but it doesn't always work out that way. I bet you know people in your church that accepted Christ when they were teenagers, and now they're in their mid-forties (or older) and you've found yourself wondering how is it that they can think or act so immaturely?

5. Don't put people in leadership just because they have a lot of past ministry experience. Your 'leadership candidate' might be a great speaker, a powerful evangelist, or one who headed up ministries in their previous church, but don't lay hands on that person just yet. Call the pastor of their former church and see what he or she has to say about this person. Why did they leave their previous church? Remember, it's easier to get them in, than it is to get them out.

19

HOW TO GO FROM 'TELLING AND SELLING', TO 'LISTENING AND LEARNING'

Most leaders tell and sell rather than listen and learn. We're always telling our people what we're going to do as a church; projects, programs, goals etc., or we're trying to sell the idea we have in order to secure their support and participation. We also do a lot of telling people what they should believe. After all, that is our job as preachers and teachers; we tell people what to believe, right?

This approach (telling and selling) has been pushed on us from the very beginning of our training to be pastors and leaders. We were told, so we tell. We were sold, so we sell. It's not entirely our fault that we turned out this way. On top of that, we're good at it. And I'm not convinced that this is altogether a bad thing, however, always telling and selling is always exhausting.

The problem is, when all your time is spent telling and selling there is little time left for listening and learning.

A leader is not so much someone out in front yelling, "Follow me.", as they are an agent of collaboration and team-building. If we want to see collaboration and team-building, we will need to learn more listening and learning skills than telling and selling skills.

You can't listen and learn until you ask your people, your leadership team, your board, or your spouse, great questions. Here are few questions that will help you listen and learn:

> What do you think?
> What do you see that I don't see?
> Do you have a better idea?
> How do you think we might better achieve our goals?
> If I have a blind spot, what do you think it might be?
> If you were in my shoes what would you do?
> Can you shoot any holes in my idea?
> Can you give me a few options?

I'm not suggesting that a leader should never tell or sell, only that, always telling and selling fails to produce

DAVE JACOBS

collaboration and team building, and, always telling and selling is always exhausting.

What are some ways that you might get better at listening and learning? Who do you need to listen to? Who do you need to learn from?

56

20

HOW TO HAVE A BLOG THAT PEOPLE WILL ACTUALLY READ

I've been blogging for over eight years now. When I started out I knew I needed to come up with a cool name for my blog, so I decided on...Dave Jacobs. I'm not sure how 'popular' my blog is. I don't follow how many visits I get, but I'm fairly certain my wife reads it since she's always pointing out to me words I've misspelled. So Ellen is one for sure.

Here are seven tips for creating a good blog, even if no one reads it.

1. Keep it short. Unless someone is unemployed, has insomnia, or is stalking you, they will probably not want to take the time to read 2000 words. The shorter the post, the more likely it is that they will read it. I try to keep mine at or under 500 words.

2. Keep it consistent. I don't know how many times I've seen pastors start a blog, post a couple of articles, and then they disappear never to be heard from again until they become unemployed, or develop insomnia. You need to post at least once a week, twice is better, if you are going to be taken seriously, especially by those who stalk you.

3. Keep it relevant. No one cares what you are interested in unless it's something they are interested in. Know who your target audience is and write to them. Scratch where people itch. (I never feel completely comfortable when I say that.)

4. Keep it honest. Give credit where credit is due. Don't steal stuff from others and make it look like it's yours, especially if it's my stuff.

5. Keep it traceable. This is related to #4. Provide links to sites that inspired you or from which you gathered your information. And in case you're mentioning studies or statistics, I will not believe you unless you point me to your source. 73% of all blog-readers dismiss undocumented data.

6. Keep it focused. If you are all over the place in your writing, you will have fewer people subscribe to your site. Develop a reputation for focusing on a limited number of subjects. For example, I typically focus on resourcing and

encouraging pastors and church leaders. And finally...

7. Let someone else have the blog that is negative, critical, judgmental, arrogant, contemptuous, and mean-spirited. There are enough of those out there, be original, be nice.

21

HOW TO AVOID OVERREACTING, UNDER REACTING, OR REACTING PREMATURELY

So let's say you suddenly have a problem on your hands, something like, a small group leader in your church is teaching some strange doctrine, or you discover that the ex-pastor that's been attending your church has been talking to other members about coming to a special meeting next Saturday at his house. Or maybe Harriett comes up to you after the service and tells you she can't stand the music, it's too loud, too contemporary, too traditional, too long, not long enough...you get the picture. And then she drops the "And I'm not the only one who feels this way." bomb. How will you react?

Great pastors don't overreact, under react, or react prematurely.

Ask yourself, "Am I overreacting?" Maybe you think you've got a problem but you don't. Maybe you think you've got a problem but the real problem is smaller than you imagine it to be. Who do you know and trust that can help you determine if you are overreacting?

Ask yourself, "Am I under reacting?" Just because you don't think you have a problem on your hands doesn't mean you don't have a problem on your hands. It's easier to look the other way and hope that the problem solves itself. Are you minimizing? Who do you know and trust that can help you determine if you are under reacting?

Ask yourself, "Am I reacting prematurely?" Maybe the situation calls for action, but when, how, and by whom? If we jump on it prematurely we might miss seeing the hand of God take care of things independent of us. Who do you know and trust that can help you determine if you are reacting prematurely?

Here's a great rule to live by: Always reflect before you react.

Very few situations demand an immediate response. Take advantage of that. Give it a day or two. Spend some time in prayer and seek wise and objective counsel. You probably don't have to respond to that nasty email within the hour after you receive it. Always reflect before you respond. You don't want to complicate things by overreacting, under reacting, or reacting prematurely.

22

HOW TO AVOID DISSONANCE, OR... HOW TO KNOW HOW PEOPLE PERCEIVE YOU

Recently I read an interesting article on the subject of 'dissonance.' Not dissonance in music (which I didn't even know there was such a thing), but dissonance in relationships.

Dissonance occurs when you think you're coming across one way, but people see you in a totally different way. Dissonance works the other way around as well, it occurs when you think you perceive someone else accurately, but the other person doesn't agree.

The author suggested that dissonance is a common culprit in marital disputes. This made me wonder how often dissonance is a common culprit in church disputes.

The author said, "The greatest single cause of dissonance is the fact that people behave their worst when they feel most powerless." Think about that. Isn't that interesting? Have you ever found that to be true with someone in your church? Have you ever found that to be true about you?

I'm always on the side of pastors. This is my bias. I know it. I think there's a need for pastors to have someone who is "on their side." But sometimes pastors are the ones to blame for relational dissonance.

Never underestimate your ability to come across in a way you didn't intend. Never underestimate your ability to choose the wrong word to use at the wrong time. Never underestimate your ability for body language and facial expressions to sabotage your relationships with others. Never underestimate your ability to contribute to dissonance.

But here's the challenge: how can you know how other people perceive you?

1. Ask God to show you how you come across to others. Yikes, but I'd rather have God hold a mirror up to my face than someone else who might just smash it over my head. And speaking of someone else...

2. Be brave enough to ask someone how they think you come across. This might hurt, but it will be worth it. You see, we don't see what we don't see and often what we don't see hurts and frustrates those around us.

Do you have someone like that in your life; someone who is for you, but at the same time will be honest with you? What if you asked someone on your broad, or someone on your leadership team, or the whole team, or your spouse, "What do you see in me that I might not see? If I had a blind spot, what might it be?"

Did I already use the word "yikes?"

23

HOW TO MINISTER WITH ONE
HAND TIED BEHIND YOUR BACK

I n April of 2016, I had the privilege of attending The
Big Little Church Conference. I shared the platform
with Karl Vaters, author of The Grasshopper Myth.
(If you haven't read his book yet, you really need to).

During one of the main sessions, I was listening to
Karl speak. I'm thinking to myself, "Man, this is good
stuff. Karl always has good stuff." But then, instead of
remaining focused on Karl, I drifted off into dream-
land, or thinkingland or some land other than where I
was sitting. The thought came to me:

"There are some pastors here, and many who were
not able to attend, who would not be able to implement the great ideas Karl was sharing because back
home, in their church, there were so many problems
and obstacles they were facing that it was like they had
one, maybe even two hands tied behind their backs."

So many pastors are trying to lead with one hand tied behind their backs. Here are some examples:

A board that is difficult to work with

An influential leader who opposes them

The threat of losing their job

A church that refuses to change

A church that is sinking financially

One or two individuals, or families, that are the ones running things and they've made that very clear

A congregation with a long history of chewing up and spitting out pastors

I bet you could add to this list.

If you feel you are trying to lead with one hand tied behind your back, let me offer these suggestions:

1. Pray. Pray for strength, pray for patience (Problems like those listed above will not go way overnight.), and pray for wisdom. Pray for the problem to be removed. If the problem is a person, pray that the person's heart be changed, or that they leave.

2. Develop a plan that will move you in the direction you need to go no matter how small that movement might be. Don't give up and accept the fact that you have one hand tied behind your back. What can be done? Any movement in the right direction, no matter how small, will eventually get you where you want to go.

What if you have two hands tied behind your back? Some of you might feel this way, and you might be right. If this is the case, you might need to move on from your present church. There are some dysfunctional and toxic churches out there that will probably never be anything other than dysfunctional and toxic. If God has called you to be a martyr then, by all means, be a martyr. But if not, move on. You must live to fight another day.

The kingdom of God needs you. However, don't make a decision as important as leaving without talking to a wise, experienced, and trusted colleague before you do anything.

24

HOW TO KNOW IF YOUR CHURCH NEEDS A CHURCH CONSULTANT

I've been coaching pastors for ten years. In addition to being a coach, I also work with churches as a consultant.

A consultant functions much like a coach to the church. Whereas a coach relates to an individual, the consultant relates to the church board, governing body, or leadership team.

A consultant comes in when a church feels stuck or in need of a fresh set of eyes to help them walk through a challenging situation. The consultant is someone objective and experienced. A consultant provides honest feedback, practical ideas, and resources that are tailor-made for the current size and specific challenges of the church.

20 Reasons why a church might benefit from a consultant:

When they feel stuck.
When considering a new direction.
When they need a fresh set of eyes.
When considering their first hire.
When considering their first church plant.
When momentum or morale is low.
When they are in decline.
When they have plateaued.
When nothing seems to be working.
When there is a need for someone to mediate conflict.
When bringing in a new pastor.
When determining the pay-package for their pastor or staff member.
When they are a new church plant.
When faced with a crisis.
When wanting to do a church diagnostic test.
When considering getting their first building.
When the leadership feels they're running out of ideas.
When preparing to set new goals for the up-coming year.

When faced with the likelihood of needing to fire or lay-off someone.
When they have a mutiny on their hands.

Is it time to bring in a consultant?

25

HOW TO CREATE DISCIPLES WHEN THEY DON'T WANT TO BE DISCIPLED

A pastor asked me, "How can I inspire people to be discipled? I've invited, offered, modeled, and even begged. No bites."

This reminds me of the story of a man taking a walk and comes upon another man hitting his head repeatedly against a wall?

"Why are you doing that?"

"Because it feels so good when I stop."

If people don't want to go deeper in their walk with Jesus there is very little we can do about it. I didn't say there is nothing we can do about it, only that there is very little we can do about it. If we assume too much responsibility for the spiritual progress of our people we might end up like that man hitting his head against a wall. Once you stop, or at least adjust your attitude, and possibly your approach, it will feel good.

To 'be discipled' implies the engagement in a process by which someone becomes a disciple. If I were coaching this pastor, I would begin by asking him, "What do you mean by 'discipled'? What does a disciple look like to you?"

If you want to make a disciple how will you know when you get one?

Begin by drawing up a list of what a disciple would look like, or be, or do. An example might be, "A disciple regularly reads their Bible, or regularly attends church, or...most important, a disciple tithes." But seriously, you get what I mean.

Don't have too many things on your list. If you have thirty-two signs of a disciple, it is doubtful that you will ever accomplish making a disciple. Limit yourself to five or six. I know, I know, that's going be hard, but try.

Now that you can see clearly what you're trying to create, draw up a list of all the things you've tried for making a disciple. What things on your list failed? Why did they fail? Is there anything on your list that worked even a little bit? Why did it work? Is there anything you'd like to try but have not tried? Why do you think this might work when the other approaches have failed?

What's preventing you from trying this new idea?

Here's something maybe you haven't tried, I call it "Building a church within a church."

Identify those people in your church that seem to be, at least somewhat, interested in going deeper in their walk with Jesus. There might only be three, or two, or only your spouse. If even your spouse isn't interested, maybe it's okay to go back to that wall.

Work with what you have, not with what you don't have. If you've only got two people interested, invite them to your home one night a week (or every other week) and begin to pray together and share together. Design this to be more of a discussion time than a teaching time. You might discuss the list you've come up with for what a disciple looks like. Don't dominate these meetings, but instead, facilitate. Slowly, slowly, slowly this will work, but it takes time and patience.

I want to end with the worse case scenario. Let's say nothing you try works. There's no one who wants to come to your house, not even your spouse. What do you do then?

Give up...for now. Stop hitting your head against that wall. Continue to pray that God would give you one person to begin with. Keep praying that the Father would stir up the hearts of your people. Keep being faithful until God tells you it's time to move on. Keep loving your people, teaching your people, and serving your people. And, even if there is no one in your church that wants to go deeper, you make sure that you are going deeper. It's hard to make disciples.

26

HOW TO TAKE YOUR
VISITORS ALL THE WAY

I don't know which is harder, getting people to come to church the first time, or getting them to come a second time. I think the second time is harder.

If someone comes back a second time, it's fair to assume that you have not scared them off yet. They liked what they experienced enough to give you a second chance. There is no guarantee that they will come back a third time, but a second time is better than no time. A second time gives us something to work with.

I want to share with you five steps to taking your first-time visitors all the way, i.e., from visitor to participant in the life of your church. What you're about the read is not rocket science. I actually know a bi-vocational pastor who is a rocket scientist, and he assured me that this is not that.

Step One: Actually, this is not so much a step as it is a reality check. It's more than likely that most visitors will not come back. But, hopefully, some will. Don't be overly discouraged if a guest does not come back. A church could have the best follow-up system in place and still experience many first-timers who never become second-timers.

Step Two: Get them through the door. What are you doing to reach new people? Regularly evaluate what is working and what is not working. Are there ways to attract new people that you've thought about but have not yet experimented with? And when talking about 'what to try,' never forget that the most effective way to attract new people is by personal invitation. What are you doing to encourage and equip your people to be inviters?

Step Three: Gather contact information. Some churches call these 'connection cards' or 'visitor cards.' You must have a way of securing their name, email, phone number and address...if they'll give it to you.

Step Four: Follow-up. Keep the initial follow-up simple. Send a quick text or email when you get home. In my last church, I would take five minutes and mail a short handwritten note. People were always impressed with this. And don't forget, once you get this information (It's hard to get some people to fill out a card the first time, but they are more likely to do so when they visit a second time.) you must file this information in a way that will be easily retrieved to be used in the future.

Step Five: Assimilate. How does your church encourage newcomers to get involved; what is your plan? In my last church our assimilation plan was three-fold:

1) Get them to come to an orientation night in our home.
2) Get them to join a small group.
3) Get them to join some type of ministry team.

Accomplishing this is easier said than done, but what is your plan?

If we want to take our visitors all the way we must:

Get them through the door.
Gather information.
Follow up with the information.
Have an assimilation plan.

How is your church doing in these four areas?

27

HOW TO SCARE AWAY VISITORS

Believe me when I say that it's harder to get a guest to come back a second time than it is the first time. You might argue with me about this, and you might be right, but certainly, we agree that it's hard to get someone back a second time. And, believe it or not, some church members aren't that keen on having new people join their church. They would never say this out loud (or maybe they would) but deep down they like the way things are, and they don't cherish the idea of new people messing things up. For those of you that are fortunate enough to pastor a church like this, here are some guaranteed ways to keep scaring your visitors away.

First, you must teach your people that being 'seeker-sensitive', or 'guest-sensitive' is what those worldly churches do while watering down the gospel to tickle people's ears.

Don't feel obligated to explain too much to your guests; after all, it's their job to figure out 'insider talk.' They should know who Bob is when you announce the men's retreat he's planning. If you do a lot of standing up and sitting down...spring it on them. It's really funny to watch people try to coordinate this with the others so they don't look like an oddball who's still sitting when others are standing. If you are one of those 'Charismatic' churches...please, please, please don't explain all the stuff going on when "the Spirit starts to move." (I can say things like this because I'm a quasi-Charismatic.)

Oh, that was funny, my auto-spell check just inserted queasy for quasi. Oh well, that works too.

I'm concerned that so many churches are no longer asking guests to stand up and introduce themselves. We need to bring this back.

Encourage your people to fellowship with their friends before and after the service, rather than try to strike up a conversation with a visitor. After all, it's easier to talk to someone you know rather than someone you don't know. If someone is looking for friends they should have brought one with them.

If your people insist on being friendly, have them be soooo friendly that it is more creepy than friendly.

Preach ten minutes too long.

While on the subject of preaching, always preach on holiness, sin, judgment, God's coming judgment, what's wrong with this sinful world, what's wrong with the liberal Christians, what's wrong with the conservative Christians, what's wrong with the Christians who can't make up their minds what they believe.

Have really bad coffee.

Have the volume of your music so loud it will make their ears bleed. People love going to a church that made them bleed.

If you use hymnals, insist on ones that have the print so small that the visitor has to squint and struggle to read the words and which results in a headache. People love going to a church that gave them a headache.

If you don't use hymnals and are one of those 'contemporary' churches that use 'choruses', choose the ones that are poorly written, hard to follow, and have really strange lyrics that even your own people don't understand, let alone those guests.

Well, that's all I've got for now. Maybe you can gather your leaders together and come up with some more ways to scare first-time visitors away. Church is for the committed and if those people were committed they would already be in your church. Who needs them anyways, unless they tithe and are willing to work in the children's ministry? We always need those people.

28

HOW TO INTERVIEW THE CHURCH THAT IS INTERVIEWING YOU

Recently a pastor asked me, "What are key questions to ask before accepting a call at a new church? And what things should we look for when we are in the process of interviewing at a church?"

What a great question. I've worked with many Pastors who are currently looking for a new church to serve in. Plus, I've worked with search committees looking for a new pastor. Want to know a secret? Most search committees don't know what they're doing, and, many pastors don't know what they are doing when looking for a new church. By this I mean that some pastors go into the interviewing process only prepared to answer questions, not to ask questions. One must remember that you are interviewing just as much as they are interviewing.

Want to know another secret? I've pastored in five churches, and none of them interviewed me. Know how I managed to escape this? Three of the five I planted, and two of the five I was simply asked to join the pastoral team by the current pastor. I know, I know, you're thinking, "You lucky bum."

In no particular order, here are some of the questions I would ask a search committee if I was candidating at a church:

> Over the past three years has the church been in decline, plateaued, or growing? To what do you attribute this?
>
> What percentage of the congregation is over fifty?
>
> How many families do you have with children in elementary school?
>
> Why did the last pastor leave?
>
> How stable is the church financially?
>
> Does the church have money in savings? What is that money used for?
>
> How are major decisions made in this church?
>
> Will I be included in the decision-making process and how?
>
> Will I be considered a member of the board and will I have a vote?
>
> Under what circumstances can I be fired?

How would you describe the morale of the leaders: high, low, or somewhere between?

To what do you attribute this?

Do you have a pastoral job description?

Is this description flexible?

What will be my salary?

Will the church provide medical insurance?

Does the church provide cost of living increases?

How are pay raises determined?

Do you have a budget that I can review?

What is the job of the church board?

Does the church have a mission, vision, or purpose statement that I can review?

Will I be expected to keep office hours and how flexible is this?

What expectations do you have for my spouse?

How much vacation time do I have each year?

How many times a year can I be out of the pulpit?

What expenses can I expect to be reimbursed for?

Does the church have a line item in the budget for books, conferences, etc.,?

What percentage of your members are volunteering at the church?

Is the population in your town or city growing, plateaued, or in decline?

To what do you attribute this?

What has this church been doing to reach and retain new people?

Do you have term-limits for board members, deacons, elders, etc.,?

What has this church done to recruit, train, and deploy new leaders?

In the past, how has this church responded to significant attempts at change?

Boy, if these questions aren't enough to scare the search committee off, nothing will. What questions might you add?

29

HOW TO HAVE A DYSFUNCTIONAL CHURCH BOARD

"My church is small."
"How small is it?"
"My church is so small that our board is my spouse and me."

That's pretty small.

Now I know that many of you reading this are blessed with an awesome church board. You couldn't be happier. Your board is made up of the most supportive, cooperative, generous, spiritual, mature people a pastor could ever hope for. I'm happy for you, I am. But you're missing out. You have no idea how faith-stretching and character-building it can be to have a dysfunctional church board. I believe one of the main ways God wants to grow you as a pastor is by using a board that drives you nuts. Therefore, let me share with you some ways you can have a dysfunctional church board.

I'm assuming that you have something to say about who joins your church board. This is not always the case. Many of you have come to an established church, and are lucky enough to have inherited a dysfunctional church board. Lucky you. The following tips will relate to both, i.e., those that have a say in choosing board members and those that don't.

First, if you have an opening that needs to be filled, try to find someone that's been in the church from the beginning. The longer a member, the better. You know the type, "I was here before you came and I'll be here after you're gone." It's board members like this that will say things every pastor loves to hear, "That's not the way we do it." or "Over my dead body." or "Wal-Mart is hiring."

When considering someone to join your board, don't worry so much about those who are spiritually mature and have proven to be loyal to you, your family, and the church. The church is a business, and the church board needs to run it like they would any business. You don't need a bunch of monks; you need business-savvy people fluent in Robert's Rules of Order.

Along these lines, let your board meetings be dominated by one outspoken, opinionated, negative, belligerent person. Every board needs to have one of these. And whatever you do, never confront them and tell them to stop it. If you do this, there is a good chance that you will indeed find out that Wal-Mart is hiring.

In your meetings have prayer make up no more than 3% of your time. More than this will encroach on all the 'business' that needs to be addressed. If someone wants to pray they can go to that prayer meeting sister Mabel has that is poorly attended. It's a win, win.

Never, I repeat, never suggest term-limits. Why would you ever want an easy way to replace a board member who causes you constant frustration?

Finally, don't worry about re-educating your church or your board as to the role of a church board. This takes a lot of time, and you still might end up at Wal-Mart. The bottom line is if it's not broke don't fix it. If it is broke, leave it alone. Remember, you've been called to be a pastor, and that has inherent in it a glutton for punishment.

30

HOW TO HAVE
A BORING SERMON

Never underestimate your ability to convince yourself that you are a great communicator when in reality you are a boring one. Here are my fifteen ways to ensure that your sermon is boring.

1. Have more than five main points to your sermon and let your church know this in advance, after all, this is what an introduction is for, i.e., to cause your people to wish they had followed their earlier inclination to stay home.

2. Seldom smile. After all, preaching is serious business, and you don't want those listening to you to think that you actually like them or enjoy preaching to them.

3. Make sure that you keep things negative. Focus on God's judgment, sin, and all the other things

that your church (or some other church) is do-ing wrong.

4. Convince yourself that you are being spontane-ous (or led by the Spirit) when in reality you are going down rabbit-trails and ever returning.

5. Whatever you do, don't rely on your notes because this is a sign that you are not led by the Spirit.

6. Don't bother rehearsing your sermon, after all, you want to be led by the Spirit.

7. Design a sermon with just a couple people in mind, that way, when they don't show up, the rest of your group can hear something that doesn't relate to them.

8. Never check with your spouse whether or not a joke is 'really' funny, or just funny to you.

9. Let your speaking voice be completely different than your normal voice. This way your people will not only be bored but will conclude that you are one person in the pulpit (or whatever it is that you stand behind, or don't stand be-hind) and a different person in normal life.

10. Use outdated sermon illustrations that you found in that sermon illustrations book that you've been using since 1982.

11. Towards the end of your sermon, tell your peo-ple that you are wrapping things up...and then don't.

12. Don't bother trying to figure out what your people would find interesting and helpful to be

taught. After all, you're in a much better position to know this than they are.

13. And the most important, let your sermon run ten minutes too long.

PASTOR'S PERSONAL LIFE

31

HOW TO KNOW IF YOU NEED
A PASTORAL COACH

A coach provides objective, honest, practical, and safe feedback while walking with you through your personal and professional challenges. My philosophy of coaching is best summed up in the following sentence: It's not my job to do your thinking for you but to help you think, help you see, help you hear what the Father is doing in your life and ministry.

Here are some reasons why you might link up with a coach.

1. If you feel stuck in an area of your personal life.
2. If you feel stuck in an area pertaining to your ministry or church.
3. If you need help in a certain ministry-skill, i.e., counseling, preaching, administration, goal-setting, etc.

4. If you are considering transitioning out of ministry or to another church.
5. If you are a new church planter.
6. If you are faced with a crisis either personal or professional.
7. If you are preparing to form your first board.
8. If you want to better your preaching skills.
9. If this is your first church as a lead pastor.

The rule of thumb is, when you feel stuck in any area of life or ministry it's good to link up with a coach.

32

HOW TO END YOUR MARRIAGE

Marriages end before marriage end. Some stay married after their marriage has ended. Being a pastor has embedded in it the potential for ruining your marriage.

Here's how to end your marriage.

Be warm and friendly and caring and attentive to your congregation but an entirely different person to your spouse. After all, it's good to have a time and place to let your defenses down. Believe me, your spouse will understand.

Having a day off is all good and fine, in theory, but in reality, a pastor needs to be available to their congregation even if it's their day off. It's important to check your email during said day, answer your phone, and read a ministry-related book. Your spouse will understand.

Never forget that nothing is more important than the church, not your children, not your marriage, not your mental and physical health...nothing. Church first, then if there is any of you left over it can be dished out to whoever is left. One of the things your spouse loves about you is your dedication to the ministry. Your spouse will understand your priorities.

Whatever you do, never make it clear to your church that your marriage and your family will always come first. Never clearly explain the boundaries you have. Remember, pastors aren't allowed to have boundaries. Your spouse will understand.

Don't establish boundaries. Your spouse will understand.

If you and your spouse are having relational problems, keep it to yourself. You can't trust anyone. You can overcome these problems on your own simply by praying more and reading your bible more. Besides, chances are that the problem is with your spouse, not you. Your spouse will understand.

Have a few unrealistic expectations for your spouse, after all, he or she is married to 'the Pastor' and congregants will expect more from them. Your spouse will understand.

Work more than forty hours a week. Fifty hours or more is better. Your spouse will understand.

Jesus didn't take vacations, why should you? Your spouse will understand.

It's best to limit your Bible reading time to when you are preparing your sermon. This will insure a shallow inner life that affects everything, including your marriage. Your spouse will understand.

Date Nights are highly overrated. Besides, when one is out two or three nights a week doing church stuff, who has time for date nights? Your spouse will understand.

Remind your spouse that driving together to midweek service is the same as a date night. Your spouse will understand.

Remind your spouse that it is their job to run interference between the children and you. When you come home after a hard day at the church, you need to be left alone and allowed to vegetate in front of the TV without any nagging pressure to pay attention to the kids. Your spouse will understand.

In conclusion, don't misunderstand me. I'm not suggesting that you actually end your marriage. You can stay married without being married. If this doesn't make sense to you, ask your spouse. Your spouse will understand.

33

HOW TO AVOID
BEING IMPULSIVE

Some pastors are impulsive. Some pastors mistake impulsiveness for the Holy Spirit. Both can get you in trouble. Impulse is defined as, 'a sudden strong and unreflective urge or desire to act.' Did you notice the word unreflective?

The longer you have been in the ministry, the more experience you have, the more training and education you've received, the greater is the chance that you will be impulsive. The reason for this is because our years of experience and training provide us with quick answers. It's the old, 'Been there, done that, I know exactly what needs to be done,' way of thinking. The tricky thing is, sometimes you're right, and sometimes you're wrong.

The more urgent a situation seems, the greater chance that you will be impulsive. Part of pastoring is putting out fires. If my house is on fire, I'm not going to sit there and reflect on what I should do. No, I'm going to grab the hose and start putting out the fire. Sometimes, in the ministry, you need to grab the hose, but many times you need to wait and assess the situation. You can think you have a fire but be mistaken. Rushing without reflecting can be like trying to put out a fire with gasoline rather than water.

Because impulsiveness can feel like the promptings of the Holy Spirit, it's easy to mistake it for the Holy Spirit. Never underestimate your ability to convince yourself, and sometimes others, that you are being led by the Spirit when you're just being impulsive.

Be cautious about any idea or action that feels impulsive. The rule is, reflective is more effective. Have someone on your team who is not afraid to tell you when they think you are being impulsive.

34

HOW TO AVOID ADULTERY
IN THE MINISTRY

A while back I was talking to a pastor about the recent news of a popular leader in his denomination who confessed to adultery. A few years ago the same denomination was rocked after finding out the same thing about two other very high-level leaders. Whenever a bomb like this is dropped, two questions start to circulate:

1. How could this have happened?
2. What can be done, if anything, to prevent this in the future?

My friend and I came up with five suggestions for avoiding emotional or physical adultery. You might want to apply them to your personal life, address them from the pulpit, or share them in a men's or women's group.

Here they are:

1. Don't think, "It could never happen to me."
2. Know the early signs of an inappropriate relationship.
3. Don't minimize or dismiss the early signs.
4. Be brutal with how you respond to the early signs.
5. Find someone you know and trust, someone who is safe, someone you could share with, who will pray with you and hold you accountable if you are ever tempted.

35

HOW TO ENCOURAGE YOURSELF

Poor Elijah. He just experienced, possibly, the highest point of his career (single-handedly, with some help from God, defeating four hundred prophets of Baal), and now he's on the run, scared to death, fleeing from the threats of Jezebel, wife of Ahab the king. (I Kings 19)

I found verse nineteen of chapter nineteen funny, "…and he went into a cave."

Do you have a tendency to retreat into a cave? Maybe it's the cave of depression or discouragement; maybe it's the cave of isolation or self-pity. For some, it is a cave of anger. Perhaps Elijah was feeling all of this. But for whatever reason, there he is, in a cave, and God tells him, "Go outside and wait for me."

First comes a great wind…but that wasn't God.

Then, an earthquake…but that wasn't God either.

Next, a fire...nope, not God. Then, a still small voice.

You know the rest of the story.

There are times when God seems to be moving in our church and times when he doesn't. But the truth is, God is always moving in our ministries. Oh it might not look like fire or a mighty rushing wind, but somewhere, somewhere you'll find the still small voice, and it sounds like…

> Someone who received direction or comfort from a word you spoke.
> Someone who is making progress in his or her faith.
> Someone who is becoming a better father or mother.
> Someone who is a little closer to Jesus than they were before they began coming to your church.

It's nice when the winds blow and the earth shakes, but the norm seems to be the little things occurring in our church that add up over months and years. Welcome the fire but rely on the whisper of God to see you through.

Why not pick up a pen and paper and draw up a list of some small things God is doing in the lives of your people and let the still small voice encourage you today.

36

HOW TO SEE YOUR BLIND SPOTS

A while ago I gave up the fight and made an appointment to see an optometrist. As much as I hated to admit it, it was time for me to get some real glasses instead of those cheap reading glasses I had relied on for the past few years.

I found the whole experience interesting. The doctor checked my vision far and near. He checked out my peripheral vision and the general health of my eye. And then he checked me for blind spots, which, to my surprise, he found. One tiny blind spot in each eye. He assured me that this was normal and almost all people have these tiny blind spots. They are just so small that you never notice them unless you're an optometrist. I would never have known that I had these blind spots unless my doctor had told me. But then again, that's the nature of blind spots; you don't see them.

We all have blind spots. Blind spots, left undetected, can be one explanation for relationship-breakdown and ineffectiveness in some areas of our ministries. It's essential that we become aware of any blind spots we might have.

One of the most important, gutsy, and helpful questions a pastor can ask someone is, "What blind spots do I have?" Now you don't want to ask this question of just anyone. But who do you know and trust? Do you know someone that loves you enough to be honest with you? I dare you to sit that person down and ask them, "In your opinion, what blind spots do you think I have?" Or, a similar question that works very well with a leadership team is, "What do you see that I don't see?"

The answers you get may be a bit hard to hear, but they will be worth it. Never underestimate the likelihood of personal blind spots, and for those blind spots to sabotage your relationships and ministry.

37

HOW TO BE MORE HUMBLE

Recently someone contacted me and asked if I could help them with their pride. The actual question was, "How can I become more humble?" This impressed me for two reasons. 1) Most people don't recognize pride in their lives, and 2) if they do, it's unlikely that they will be brave enough, or humble enough, to seek out help.

So I got to thinking. What practical things could we do that would lead us towards humility? I came up with four ways to become more humble; they are: talk less, do less, reveal less, and invest more.

1. **Talk less.** Giving up the need to have an opinion, an answer, or a solution for everything, is a nice break from the pressure we feel to have an opinion, an answer, or a solution for everything. There is a reason why many from monastic traditions took vows of silence. They believed that by

merely talking less, one could experience God more, and experience the humility that pleases Him. It has always been my opinion that pastors talk too much, and I should know, I was one.

2. **Do less.** So often we derive our sense of value by what we do, i.e., our job or ministry. A full schedule, at least in our minds, validates our existence and says to those who observe us, "Look how busy I am, I'm so important." It's not unusual for a pastor whose schedule is too full, to be driven by pride and not even realize it. In addition to this, we worry about what people think, and wonder if they ever question whether or not we are doing our job? Do less but make sure what you do is more focused and effective.

3. **Reveal less.** Avoid every opportunity to draw attention to yourself or your accomplishments, by this I mean, any form of subtle boasting. It's amazing how easy it is for us to sneak self-flattery into our conversations.

4. **Invest more** time alone with Jesus. When we spend time in silence and solitude with our Lord, the meek and humble Jesus rubs off on us. His character slowly changes our character, especially in the area of pride.

So if we want to be more humble, a good place to start will be to talk less, do less, reveal less, and invest more time alone with Jesus.

38

HOW TO STAY MARRIED
IN THE MINISTRY

Ellen and I have been married 38 years. We've pastored five churches, three of which we planted. Somewhere along the line, we had five children all of who are now responsible Christian adults and have given us ten delicious (as Ellen likes to describe them) grandchildren. Wow! As you can imagine, there are some things we've learned about pastoring and the pressure this puts on a marriage. One wise old pastor once confessed that he had only two goals in life: to stay a Christian and to stay married. Here are some tips for staying married while ministering.

1. Don't encourage after-hour phone calls from your parishioners. A good rule of thumb says,

unless it's bleeding or burning, it can probably wait until tomorrow. Never tell your people that they can call you anytime they feel like it. Believe me, if they really want to talk to you they will call anyway, but we don't need to encourage this, and you don't need to pick up. Screen your calls. Similarly, never tell your people that they can drop by anytime.

2. Only work an appropriate number of hours. Nowhere in the Bible does it say pastors have to work forty hours a week. Just because some of your people work forty or more hours a week doesn't mean you have to. Here's a good formula:

a) If you are full-time at the church, plan for a thirty-hour workweek. You know an extra ten hours will creep in somehow and you'll probably end up putting in forty anyway. The thing is, if you plan on a forty-hour workweek, and the extra ten creeps in, now you're up to fifty hours a week, and that's too much to maintain a healthy marriage.

b) If you are part-time at the church (bi-vocational) never plan more than a twenty-hour workweek.

c) If you work full-time outside of the church never plan more than a ten to fifteen-hour workweek.

3. Take vacations.
4. Take two days off a week. If your spouse works, make sure your days off coincide with theirs.
5. When at home, have something to talk about other than the church.
6. Never become emotionally attached to someone of the opposite sex.
7. If your marriage is in trouble, get help. There is no shame in going to a marriage counselor. There is shame in your marriage falling apart. Another rule to live by: If one of you thinks you need to see a counselor, you need to see a counselor. Just go. And remember, never talk to someone of the opposite sex about your marriage problems unless it's a professional counselor.
8. Make time for sex.
9. Always remember, your marriage is more important than your church.
10. Try to find some friends outside of the church. Another couple in the ministry is ideal.
11. Invest in the care of your soul. There will be a direct correlation between how happy your marriage is and how consistent and meaningful your times of solitude and silence are.

Pastoring a church can be hard on a marriage. It would be an interesting conversation for you to sit down with your spouse and go over these 11 tips and discuss how your marriage measures up.

39

HOW TO TURN IRRITATION INTO SOMETHING HELPFUL

Did you know that pearls owe their existence to irritation? A pearl is the product of a species of oysters and other shellfish, formally called 'bivalve mollusks.' A pearl is formed when irritants become lodged in the soft tissue inside an oyster's shell, and, to protect itself, the oyster produces a coating around the irritant. This coating, called 'nacre', builds up in thin layers and creates an iridescent cover over the irritant. The resulting product is a pearl.

Natural, or wild pearls, are very rare, and, therefore, much more expensive than cultured or manufactured pearls. A manufactured pearl is one that has been pried open and a small piece of shell is implanted (an irritant). The oyster is closed back up and in about six months, voila...you've got a pearl!

What is currently irritating you? Is it circumstances beyond your control? Is it a lack of resources, volunteers, or finances? Is it a person you work with, live with, or go to church with? Who or what is your source of irritation?

I wonder how often irritation is random, and how often it is by design. Like the manufacturer of cultured pearls, God often pries us open and implants an irritant in order to produce a pearl. It might take a while to discover the pearl, and of course, we can spit the irritant out, and miss the pearl altogether.

I have come to believe that inside every irritation is a potential pearl. Now go back to the source of irritation that came to you a few moments ago. Ask yourself:

> What might the Father be trying to say to me through this irritation?
> What lesson might God be attempting to teach me from that irritating person?
> Are there any ways that I might have contributed to the problem?
> I wonder who it is that I might be irritating?
> Is there anything I can do about that?

40

HOW TO RECOGNIZE, ADMIT, AND RESPOND TO FEAR

P astors are constantly dealing with fear.
A while back I began to notice how often pastors make decisions or take actions, that are motivated by fear.

When I was pastoring there were many things I feared, some of them I was conscious of, and others not.

> I was afraid of losing people.
> I was afraid of people not liking me.
> I was afraid of loosing my job.
> I was afraid of loosing my paycheck.
> I was afraid of a bad offering.
> I was afraid of the church failing.
> I was afraid of making a significant mistake.

> I was afraid of my marriage suffering
> because of the ministry.
> I was afraid of my children suffering be-
> cause of the ministry.
> I was afraid of my soul suffering because
> of the ministry.

If any of these fears are yours, I don't blame you. Most of our fears have at least some legitimacy to them. In my opinion, the list above contains legitimate fears.

I know, I know...Jesus said, "Fear not", but we do.

Not only is fear an unpleasant burden to live under, fear also affects how we lead, and the decisions we make or don't make. It's hard to think clearly when you are fearful. It's hard to hear from God when your ears are plugged up with fear.

So what's a pastor to do? What steps might one take to loosen the power of fear?

First, admit to yourself that you are afraid, and then tell a trusted friend. It's good to hear you say to yourself, "I'm afraid of..." It's good to hear yourself tell someone else, "I've noticed that I'm afraid of..." And real victory begins when we admit to God that we have fears.

There is something freeing about admitting our weaknesses.

Next, bring the specific fears to Jesus in prayer.

"Don't be fearful, but instead, bring all your fears to the Lord in prayer, and don't forget to be thankful.

When you bring your worries and fears to God, your heart will be filled with a peace so great it's hard to describe. All of this is from Jesus, who will watch over your heart and emotions." (Phil. 4:6,7)

I don't want to be simplistic. The stronger the fear, the harder it can be to defeat it. But here's the thing, notice the connection Paul makes between prayer and peace? Through solitude and prayer, we will find peace, courage, faith, wisdom, and healing for the things we are afraid of.

Fear can be weakened. Fear can be overcome. It might take some time for prayer to 'work, ' but prayer works. Keep bringing your fears to Jesus.

The Father doesn't want your soul or your ministry to be weighed down with fear. Take the steps necessary to move away from fear. You can do it!

41

HOW TO ADMIT YOUR LIMITATIONS WITH PASTORAL COUNSELING

I doubt that Lt. Harry Callahan had even an ounce of pastoral gifting, and normally I would not turn to someone known as Dirty Harry (I'm assuming you're familiar with the movie I'm referring to.) for advice on pastoral counseling, but I have to admit that one of the best things I've ever learned about counseling I learned from this character played by the legendary Clint Eastwood. One line…one simple line in the movie: "A man's gotta know his limitations." Thank you Dirty Harry.

If you're like most pastors, you know that pastoral counseling can take up a lot of your time. Most would agree that this is part of our job. But the next time you're ready to recommend Cloud and Townsend's book, Boundaries, make sure you're comfortable with some boundaries of your own. After all, "A man's gotta know his limitations."

Be willing to admit if a person's problem is out of your league. Some problems are best left to the professional Christian counselor.

Don't be too quick to agree to meet with a person long-term. If the person's problem is such that they need long-term counseling, they probably need a professional.

Agree to meet with the person one time to adequately understand what it is they are dealing with and to be able to diagnose the best way to address it. Sometimes people think they need pastoral counseling when they need professional Christian counseling and vice-versa. Often a person might think they need to meet with you for the next seven months, when one or two sessions could be enough. I never agreed to anything with the person who approaches me for counseling beyond the first meeting.

If your pastoral plate is already full, say so. I know we never want to turn someone away, but there can be times when we need to say, "Right now I just don't have the time to do counseling." If you find yourself in a busy season, try to have a list of referrals ready (lay or professional) that you could give the person so that they can get help if they really want to pursue counseling.

Some ministers love counseling and some don't. Some are good at it, some poor at it, and many somewhere in-between. Counseling comes with the job, but sometimes it's best to pass, or pass off. Don't feel bad referring someone to a professional. Don't be afraid to admit that their situation is too complicated for you to handle. There's nothing wrong with admitting you simply don't have the time to meet with the person long term. And don't forget the words of our good friend Dirty Harry, "A man's gotta know his (or her) limitations."

42

HOW TO RESPOND WHEN THERE IS A PROBLEM THAT YOU CONTRIBUTED TO

When I was pastoring I had my fair share of frustrations with certain leaders:

Maybe they were consistently late to meetings.

Maybe they skipped too many Sunday mornings.

Maybe they didn't do what they said they'd do.

Maybe they were called leaders, but they weren't leading anything.

Maybe they were always negative.

Maybe they thought the church is going to hell in a handbasket.

Maybe they challenged every good idea I came up with.

Maybe they talked about me behind my back.

Maybe they were the first to leave after service on Sundays.

Maybe they weren't very friendly to guests.

I'm sure you could easily add to this list.

If you are frustrated with a leader, the problem is either with them, with you, or a combination of the two.

Before you do anything, ask yourself questions such as:

Is there any way in which I might have contributed to this problem?

Are there any expectations I have that the leader might be unaware of?

Have I spoken to them already, or have I been holding in my frustration and now it has grown into something bigger than when it started?

Has my frustration crossed the line and is now anger?

What response to them might I give that would bring the most pleasure to Jesus?

Never underestimate your ability to be a contributor to the problem but convince yourself that blame rests solely on the other person.

43

HOW TO REGAIN THE CONFIDENCE OF YOUR PEOPLE

When a church is doing well and growing, people's confidence in their pastor increases. This may be warranted, and maybe not. When a church is struggling or not growing, people's confidence in their leader decreases. This may be warranted, and maybe not.

What do I mean by "may be warranted, and maybe not?"

Very few people know why their church is growing or why their church is shrinking. They think they know, but usually their explanations are naive and simplistic. Ask your normal parishioner why they think their church is growing and they might attribute it to dynamic worship, or great preaching, or small groups, or the youth ministry. Ask your normal parishioner why they think their church is in decline and they might mention that their church can't offer the same ministries as the big church down the street, or their building isn't attractive, or the pastor is not that dynamic of a preacher.

Now it's true, some pastors are better leaders than other pastors. Some pastors are better preachers, visionaries, better at leadership development, have better people-skills than others. But here's the thing; it's rare that a church is growing, or in decline, and the reason for this is solely because of the pastor. And this is especially true when a church is shrinking.

Still, when a church is struggling, or not growing, it's not unusual for the people's confidence in their pastor to decrease. How then, might one regain the confidence of their people?

1. Occasionally teach on the dynamics of church growth and church decline, i.e., the reasons why some churches grow and others don't. Make sure you mention that for the most part, growth and decline can be a mystery.

2. If your church is in decline, don't ignore it, sweep it under the rug, or put a spin on it. You don't want to give your people the impression that you've got your head buried in the sand.

3. If your church is in decline, gather a few of your best people and try to figure out what's going on. I often tell pastors, "Do you have a big P

problem or a little p problem? Do you have a Problem or a problem?"

A capital P problem is when you know people are leaving because they are unhappy, disgruntled...and sharing this with others. A lowercase p is decline due to members moving out of the area or the normal attrition every church experiences, even that big church down the road.

4. Every once in a while your people need to hear that our focus and fascination with numbers and church growth is mostly a North American mindset and not necessarily a Biblical mindset.

5. Evaluate if you have any 'health-inhibitors.' I help pastor with this all the time. 'Health-Inhibitors' are things we are doing or not doing that could be sabotaging our attempts to grow a healthy church. Correcting said inhibitors is no guarantee that your church is going to start growing numerically, but it doesn't hurt, and you have more control over church health than you do church growth.

44

HOW TO STAY ON TOP OF IT ALL

I have a long list of things I value, things I want to do, things I need to do. Some of the things on my list are time-sensitive, but most are not. An appointment with a pastor is time-sensitive. Getting to that book on Ignatius of Loyola is not. I don't forget things that are time-sensitive. Those that aren't, well, that can be a different story.

I wouldn't say I'm a procrastinator; I prefer to think of myself as a "Free-Selective." (Don't bother to 'Google' it, I just now made it up.) As a Free-Selective, I feel a freedom to select what I give my time to and what not to. Sounds good, doesn't it? But I must confess, I've come to realize I can be a poor Free-Selective. You see, I tend to gravitate towards those things I enjoy doing or those that are easy to do, and end up neglecting the rest of the things on my list.

Are you a Free-Selective?

If you're tired of feeling frustrated all the time because you are neglecting so many important things, here's something you can try.

Divide your days into blocks of time. Each block of time is reserved for certain things. Only allow yourself to do those specific things during their allotted block of time. For example, you might have a block of time reserved for administration, another one for returning phone calls and emails. You could have a block of time for study, or reading, or planning. Get it?

You know what you'll discover? At the end of each day, you'll feel pretty good about what you have accomplished. You'll be giving time to everything on your list, not just those things you enjoy giving time to. Because of this, it will be easier to take off your 'Pastor hat' at the end of the day and allow yourself to enjoy 'you-time' and 'family-time' without being distracted by all the stuff you're not staying on top of.

> Do you want to read more? Schedule it!
> Do you find yourself needing time to think and reflect? Schedule it!
> Do you want meaningful time with your spouse or kids? Schedule it!

Schedule what you value and need in order to be healthy, happy, and responsible. Guard that time as you would any other appointment you might make. I guarantee you'll feel less overwhelmed and experience more balance and peace in your life and ministry.

45

HOW TO AVOID EMAIL-REGRET

It was the early 90's and I was banging out sermon notes on my Royal typewriter. The phone rings and it's one of the men from my church. He starts telling me how much I need a computer. I thought to myself, "What would I ever do with a computer?" But he persisted, and even offered to buy me one, which he did. And with that, I entered the computer-age.

There was about a six-month learning curve that almost resulted in divorce since I shut myself up in my home office, refusing to let anyone in who might interfere with my attempts to master all the software programs that came pre-loaded with my new computer. I was mesmerized, hypnotized, possessed by this little box sitting on my desk. (My first computer was a Mac Classic.) Before I knew it, I could not imagine what life was like before I owned one.

Computers have become a major part of our lives. Computers have opened up a whole new world of communication: Facebook, Twitter, etc., and of course, email. Email is a great tool, but sometimes it can get us in trouble.

Here are five ways to avoid email-regret.

1. If someone sends you a nasty email criticizing you or the church, never, let me repeat, never respond until the next day.
2. Before you reply, run your response past your spouse. If your husband or wife recommends omitting or adding something, take their advice. Almost without exception, every time I've violated these first two tips I've regretted it.
3. Always remember that email can't communicate your tone or facial expressions. These are important components that can make or break effective communication. An emoticon might help, but it's seldom as good as the real thing.
4. Some communication is best done in person. Some is best done over the phone. Some can be handled in an email or letter. Have someone in your life that can help you decide which is best.
5. In regards to email and all forms of communication, remember Dave's Rule: Never underestimate your ability to be misunderstood. And another pretty good is, Never underestimate your ability to think you're being clear when all the while being vague.

46

HOW TO CHOOSE A GREAT BOOK
FOR SPIRITUAL FORMATION

Next to the comfortable chair I sit on when spending time with God, is my stack of 'quiet-time tools.' I have a Bible, a notebook for journaling, and a notebook for writing my prayers. I have a small pad of paper to write things down that I don't want to forget, things that might pop into my mind and distract me. In addition to these, I always have a book I am reading devotionally for spiritual formation. Some of these books are considered spiritual classics, and some of them have been written by contemporary authors who focus on the inner-life. Francis Bacon wrote, "Some books are to be tasted, others are to be swallowed, and some few to be chewed and digested."

DAVE JACOBS

Over the years there have been many books that I have chewed and digested for the purpose of spiritual formation. Here are some examples:

> A Monk's Alphabet, by Jeremy Driscoll
> The Seeking Heart, by François Fénelon
> The Practice of the Presence of God, by Brother Lawrence
> Devotional Classics, Selected Readings for Individuals and Groups, edited by Richard Foster and James Bryan Smith
> Any volume from the 'Rekindling the Inner Fire' series, edited by David Hazard
> Shepherds Balm, by Richard Earl
> The Wisdom of the Desert, arranged by Thomas Merton
> My Utmost for His Highest, by Oswald Chambers
> A Simple Path, by Mother Teresa
> The Essential Wisdom of the Saints, edited by Carol Kelly-Gangi

For the really, really serious reader:

> Interior Castle, by Saint Teresa of Avila
> Dark Night of the Soul, by Saint John of the Cross

Experiencing the Depths of Jesus Christ,
by Jeanne Guyon

My two favorite books on the spiritual disciplines:

Celebration of Discipline, by Richard
Foster
The Life You've Always Wanted, by John
Ortberg

My favorite spiritual writer of all time is Thomas
Merton. In all my years of reading, no single writer has
had more influence on my spiritual formation than
Thomas Merton. Merton said, "For there are people
one meets—in books and in life—with whom a deep
resonance is at once established" and their books "open
up a new road" for you." For some reason, Merton has
been one of those people for me.

If you are unfamiliar with Merton, the book Seeds,
edited by Robert Inchausti, is a great introduction to his
writings, and is, in itself, a great book to use devotionally. I always recommend Seeds to those who want to start
reading Merton. When Merton was alive he endorsed A
Thomas Merton Reader for those interested in getting to
know him and his work. Both are excellent introductions.

Here are some helpful questions to ask to determine if a book is a spiritual classic or a book that fo-
cuses on spiritual formation:

Does this book have anything to do with church growth, church management, pastoral skills, philosophy of ministry, biblical commentary, Greek or Hebrew word study, or leadership development? If so, it's not what I'm talking about.

Does this book have an obvious focus on spiritual formation, spiritual disciplines, personal intimacy with God or going deeper in one's relationship with God? If so, then it probably is what I'm talking about.

Is the book trying to make you more knowledgeable or more spiritual? If the focus is more on education than formation, then it's not what I'm talking about.

Is the author still living? If so, then there's a 50/50 chance it's not a spiritual classic.

Do you read more for education, recreation, or inspiration? What type of input do you need more of: education, recreation, or inspiration? Which books on the recommended reading list have you read? Which books on the list would are you interested in reading? Which of these could you buy today?

What's stopping you from buying it?

47

HOW TO LIMIT
OFFENDING PEOPLE

Never underestimate your ability to offend. People are easily offended, and sometimes we can be easily offensive. You put those two things together and you've got trouble. The writer of Proverbs put it this way, "It's easier to break into a fortified city than to regain trust and loyalty once it's been lost because you offended a person." (Proverbs 18:19)

I know, I know, some of you might be thinking, "But speaking the truth will offend people. The gospel is offensive: I Corinthians 1:23 and Galatians 5:11. Besides Jesus offended people: Matthew 13:57 and Mark 6:3."

That's not the type of offense I'm talking about.

I'm referring to an offense that is not necessary, or one that could be avoided. There is an offense that comes because we've said or done something stupid or insensitive. Why would I want to offend someone if

I didn't need to? If I need to I need to, but if I don't, why would I want to? Four times the scriptures tell me to avoid offending or placing a stumbling block before people: I Corinthians 8:9 and 10:32, II Corinthians 6:3, and Romans 14:13.

I remember listening to a pastor at a conference say, "The only way not to offend people is to say nothing, do nothing, and be nothing." The people around me burst into applause and cheers, but I could not help but think that some had interpreted this as permission to offend.

Some pastors offend because they have been offended, and this is their way of striking back. I wish Paul hadn't said, "Don't return evil for evil.", but he did. (Romans 12:17)

Despite my greatest efforts, I'm still going to (hopefully unintentionally) offend someone. Is it possible to limit the times I offend others?

Ask yourself these four 'offense-limiting' questions before you say or do anything that has the potential of being offensive:

1. How might my words or actions offend this person?
2. Do I care if I offend them?
3. Should I care if I offend them?
4. Can I achieve my objective in a way that might be less likely to offend?

A good rule to live by: If you have to ask yourself if what you're about to say or do will be offensive, it will probably be offensive.

48

HOW TO RESPOND WHEN YOU'VE ALREADY OFFENDED SOMEONE AND THEY'VE LET YOU KNOW IT

1. Resist the temptation to become defensive and justify your actions.
2. In prayer and quiet reflection, ask the Father to show you how you contributed to the offense.
3. Apologize without any explanations or qualifiers. Examples of poor apologies:

   "I'm sorry that you were offended but…"
   "I apologize but…"

A good rule to live by in regards to apologizing is: If you use the word 'but' you'll come off as a 'butt.' What's an example of a good apology?

"I'm sorry that I _____." PERIOD! Stop right there! Don't say another word!

You might be saying to yourself, "Yeah, but it wasn't all my fault. They needed to hear this." You might be right. But you will probably have an opportunity to re-visit whatever it is you think they needed to hear. Do your best to clear the air and approach the matter an-other day in another way.

A good rule to remember: An offended person will not objectively listen to anything you have to say to them until after, and maybe not even then, the offense has been cleared up.

Some final thoughts about people who we've offended:

I was once told, "An offended person can never re-ally be a loyal person." I know that sounds pessimistic and seems to discount the ability of Jesus to change a person's heart, but apart from a 'heart-change,' I think I would agree.

It takes a mature Christian to truly walk away from offense and embrace trust and faith in the person that offended them. Plus, some people are offended and they don't realize it. But eventually, like poking a sleep-ing dog, something is going to poke them and they're going to wake up and bite you.

Almost all relational conflict can be traced back to an offense. Most church splits can be attributed to somebody offending somebody, and the person offended didn't deal with it in a mature way, so it builds and builds and builds until it erupts in division.

Be cautious about putting someone in a leadership position if you had a serious disagreement with him or her in the past and it was never really addressed and dealt with. If a person was offended once they probably will be again.

Few people deal with their offense so well that they can move on unaffected by it in the future.

A good friend and great pastor in southern California, Steve Mason of Oasis Church, emailed me with a fascinating tidbit:

"I didn't want to put a long post on Facebook so I'm emailing you. I saw your post about offense. The Greek word for offense is the word "scandalon." It's where we get the English word scandal. Interestingly enough, the small metal piece on a mousetrap where you put the cheese is called a scandalon. The picture is obvious, offense is a trap. If you take the bait and become offended, you are the one who ends up being trapped."

I couldn't help but turn this around and think about how many churches have been trapped in stunted growth, conflict, and disunity, because of one or two offended people in the church who slowly spread their toxic attitude throughout the fellowship.

49

HOW TO RESPOND WHEN SOMEONE HAS OFFENDED YOU

What should I do when I have been offended? First of all, welcome to the club. Unless we learn how to deal constructively with being offended it will be impossible for us to stay the course and finish well. The word 'offensive' can be translated 'stumbling block,' and all pastors have skinned knees and stubbed toes. Having said that…

1. Prayerfully ask the Father how you might have contributed to the relational breakdown between you and the person who has offended you.
2. If there is any way in which you have been wrong, then humbly make restitution.

3. Can you think of anything the Father might want to teach you by allowing this offense to have occurred?
4. Prayerfully ask the Father if you are overreacting or have misunderstood the person?
5. Bring your feelings of offense to the Father and wait upon him for peace and healing.

50

HOW TO AVOID DEATH BY MINISTRY

Someone once said, "I'll have plenty of time to rest when I get to heaven." That might be true, and not taking time to rest just might get you there quicker.

When one pastor was challenged about his sixty-hour workweek, he said, "Well, I'd rather burn out than rust out."

Me? I'd rather do neither.

Let me ask you a few questions.

1. Do you have more than one day off a week?
2. Do you work more than forty hours a week?
3. Are you gone more than two nights a week doing ministry related things?
4. How many hours of sleep do you get each night?
5. Do you observe a personal Sabbath?

6. How many weeks a year do you take off for vacation?

7. Do you have a consistent and meaningful devotional life?

8. How often do you get away alone with your spouse?

9. On a scale of 1 to 10 (1 = lowest), how stressed do you feel?

10. On a scale of 1 to 10, how busy do you feel?

11. Does your spouse feel you are working too little, too much, or just right?

12. On a scale of 1 to 10, how much margin is there in your week, your month, and your life?

I hope you do get to rest once you get to heaven, but your loved ones don't want you to get there prematurely. It's better to neither burn out or rust out. What adjustments could you make in your life to move you towards more rest? What small thing could you start with?

51

HOW TO AVOID PLAYING GOD

Think about how often you give advice. It's what pastors do. We are professional advice-givers. Our preaching is filled with advice. Our pastoral counseling is filled with advice. The meetings we lead are filled with our advice.

This isn't necessarily a bad thing. Jesus gave advice. The writers of the New Testament gave advice. Advice-giving is not wrong it's just, for many pastors, a default, something we revert to automatically.

When advice-giving is our default, there is a good chance that we are not listening deeply to the person who has come to us. Instead of fully listening, we're only half-listening while formulating our response (advice) we're waiting to give as soon as the person stops talking.

When advice-giving is our default, we fail to help those who come to us learn how to think for themselves.

When advice-giving is our default, we reinforce in others a dependency on us rather than God. It's easier for them to come to us and get advice rather than prayerfully seek God for his advice.

When we give advice, we're playing God.

What if our default was not advice?

What if our default was to ask great questions that helped our people think for themselves?

What if the advice we gave to those who come to us for advice was, "Spend the next week in prayer, and we'll meet to discuss what you discovered."

What if the advice we gave to those who come to us for advice was, "Spend the next week studying the scriptures to see if the Bible has any advice of its own for you? Then let's get together, and you can share with me what you found?"

What if we gave advice as a last resort, rather than a first resort?

What if we stopped playing God all the time?

52

HOW TO AVOID MISTAKES
WHEN UNDER PRESSURE

Pressure and decision-making seldom mix well. Pastoring means pressure. Pastoring means making important decisions. So, pastoring + pressure + decision-making = trouble.

Be careful about making decisions while under stress or pressure. If you are in a 'bad place,' i.e., stressed, burned out, angry, etc., hold off on making any important decisions. If someone in your church comes up to you with some problem and demands that you act immediately...wait, don't be pressured into action because something seems urgent to someone else. When we make decisions under pressure or stress, the 'mistake factor' rises significantly.

Five rules for decision-making:

1. Never make an important decision alone.
2. Never make an important decision without seeking objective counsel.
3. Never make an important decision without including your spouse.
4. Never make an important decision when under stress or pressure.
5. Most problems are not as urgent as they might seem. Therefore, you can wait to make most decisions.

I believe it was Charles E. Hummel who coined the phrase, "tyranny of the urgent" and wrote a great little book on the subject. Don't be bullied. Don't be pressured by situations that seem to demand that you act immediately. If you are under stress or feeling pressured...wait.

53

HOW TO TURN YOUR KIDS AWAY FROM THE CHURCH

Pastoring can take a toll. Pastoring can take a toll on your devotional life. Pastoring can take a toll on your marriage. And Pastoring can take a toll on your children.

When your children are young, it's easy to keep them interested in church. The test of our parenting isn't whether or not our children love to go to church, or VBS, or summer camp. The test is what they think about the church when they become teenagers, and more so, when they become young adults and venture out on their own. There are too many PK's out there who want nothing to do with the church.

Here are nine ways to ensure your children turn away from their faith and the church,

1. Act differently at church than you do at home.
2. Be away from your family more than two nights a week doing ministry related activities.
3. Tell your children that you expect more from them because their father is a pastor.
4. Invest at least fifty to sixty hours a week in church work so that you will be exhausted and spent by the time you get home. This way you will insure that your family gets your leftovers, rather than you at your best.
5. When sharing problems at the church with your spouse, make sure to speak loud enough for your young children to overhear.
6. Neglect your devotional times so that you are handling the pressures of life and ministry in your own strength. Whenever this is the norm, the first to suffer is our family.
7. Don't worry too much about having a day off (and remember a true day off means nothing happening that has anything to do with ministry) or vacation time.
8. Give out your personal phone number and let your people know that they can call you anytime they want. Remember, you're a pastor 24/7. When the phone rings, even if you are reading your children a book, stop and answer the phone. Ministry comes first.

9. Remember your priorities: Church, spouse, children, and your soul.

Having said all this, a ministry couple can do all the right things and still have a child that turns away from the church and Jesus. It happens. It's sad. But do your best and pray, pray, pray.

54

HOW TO HAVE REALISTIC VS. UNREALISTIC EXPECTATIONS

You've heard it before, "Set the bar high. People will rise to the level of your expectations." Or, "Expect great things from God."

To be honest with you, and please don't burn me at the stake for heresy, I'm not sure such statements are always true.

One reason why we experience frustration and disappointment in the ministry is due to unrealistic expectations. You can have unrealistic expectations for your people, and you can have unrealistic expectations for God. Let's start with God.

An unrealistic expectation for God is when we expect God to do something that He hasn't clearly promised to do. Now, granted, Christians will differ on what God has promised in the Bible and what He hasn't. Based on your theology, or hermeneutics, or denomination, you might think one thing is a promise to expect God to fulfill, while another pastor might think differently. But what I'm referring to are the many voices (usually pastors of large churches) that tell us things like...

> God wants your church to grow.
> God wants to use you to reach your city for Jesus.
> If you want to grow your church, so you need to focus on _____ or _____ or_____.
> God wants to do great things in your ministry and through your church.

I kind of believe those statements, but the problem is that such statements revolve around formulas and numbers. Formulas don't always work. Numbers don't always indicate church health.

There are more ways for a church to grow than merely by numbers. A church might grow in numbers but very, very slowly. I haven't heard of a church that has successfully "reached its city for Jesus." Why is it that "great things" are seldom "small things?" If formulas work, then why are there so many churches that have implemented the formulas and still are not experiencing numerical growth?

What are you believing God for? What are you expecting Him to do for you? What are you basing that on? If you are convinced that your expectations are based on the scriptures then fine, hold on to those promises. But if not, rethink your expectations.

And what about the expectations we have for our people?

If you expect your people to be as 'into it' as you are, then you are setting yourself up for disappointment. If by raising the bar of commitment, you have seen your people leap up and over that bar like Superwoman (or man), then good for you, congratulations, you've accomplished something most pastors never experience. I'm not exactly suggesting that we lower our expectations...but maybe I am.

Maybe it's more about having realistic expectations than unrealistic ones. And to be honest with you, some of the pastors I interact with have unrealistic expectations, and that is why they are so discouraged, frustrated, and lack peace and joy in the ministry. In regards to goals, I have a saying, "Set the bar so low that you can't help but step over it."

Don't stop praying and planning to reach new people for Jesus. Ask God to do great things with your church, just be careful how you define 'great.' Be content without becoming complacent. If you want to have more peace, discover those unrealistic expectations you have with God and your people, and adjust them accordingly.

VISION, DIRECTION & DISCERNMENT

55

HOW TO HAVE A VISION FOR
YOUR CHURCH THAT SUCCEEDS

The dictionary defines 'vision' as, "the faculty or state of being able to see, the ability to think about or plan the future with imagination or wisdom."

Let me ask you, how's your vision?

A while back, I needed to see my Optometrist. It had been a few years. My glasses weren't working as well as they should. Well actually, it was my eyes that weren't working as well as they should. My vision was failing. Nothing drastic, only what's to be expected as one gets older. All I needed was a slight adjustment to my prescription, order some new glasses, and I was good to go. No more squinting.

It's not unusual for a person to have to stay on top of their vision as they get older. The same is true of a church, or a pastor. We've all read those articles on 'vision.' Maybe you've attended a conference on "Getting your vision for the coming year." And I know you're familiar with that often pulled out of context verse, "Without vision the people perish."

In the church world, when we talk about 'vision,' we mean the ability to think about or plan the future with imagination, wisdom, or, hopefully, the leading of the Holy Spirit. Vision is the mental image of what the future of your church will or could be. Here are five reasons why your vision might fail.

1. **Multiple vision.** I remember hearing someone say, "The problem with the church today is not a lack of vision, but multiple vision." What they meant was that often in a church there would be too many ideas as to where the church should be headed. If everyone is not on the same page, you will be frustrated while trying to lead in a direction some don't want to go in. How unified is the vision of your church? Is everyone on board and paddling in the same direction?

2. **You don't see it clearly.** I believe that vision starts with the pastor. I'm not saying that your leaders don't play any part in developing and implementing the vision of your church, but I do believe, for the most part, that vision begins with the pastor. If you are not clear on the direction of your church, don't be surprised if what

you see (fuzzy as it may be) fails to get traction. Do you see where you want to go clearly?

3. **You can't articulate the vision clearly and simply.** I think it was Albert Einstein who said something like, "If you can't describe something in a simple way, you don't really understand the thing you are trying to describe." Until you can articulate your vision well enough for a fifth-grader to grasp, you'd better hold off.

4. **You haven't secured 'buy-in.'** Remember to give your leaders and the rest of your church, at least as much time to buy into your vision as it took you to develop your vision. I see this all the time. The leader has been working on the vision for weeks, maybe for months. Finally, they're done. They're excited to share it at their next leadership/board meeting, but when they do, they are met with blank stares, objections, or initial rejection. They go home discouraged and defeated. But the problem often is not their stiffed-necked, visionless, hard-hearted, reluctant to change leaders...it's simply that they needed more time to process, to think, to question, to chew on things for a while. These things take time.

5. **A failure to program around the vision.** You might see it clearly. You might be able to articulate it simply and clearly. Everybody might

be on the same page. But if you don't program around the vision, it will never be anything other than a nice idea on paper. To program around vision, ask these questions:

a) What do we need to start doing to see our vision succeed?

b) What are we doing that we need to do more of in order to see our vision succeed?

c) Is there anything we need to do less of to see our vision succeed?

Are you suffering from multiple vision?

Do you see your vision clearly?

Can you articulate it simply and clearly?

Have you allowed enough time for everybody to get on board?

Do your programs move your church towards your vision or away from your vision?

56

HOW TO MAKE SURE YOU'RE NOT MISTAKING WHAT GOD WANTS, FOR WHAT YOU WANT

Never underestimate your ability to mistake what you want, for what God wants.

"Delight yourself in God and He will give you whatever is in your heart." Psalms 37:4

Well, not exactly.

I think He will give you what you want as long as He wants the same thing. I have discovered that sometimes God disguises His answer and makes it look like something other than what we asked for. We think He said "no" to our request when in fact, He said "yes," but it looked different than we expected. And have you noticed that He often doesn't give us what we ask for when we ask for it? It's easy to mistake 'wait' for 'no.'

All that to say, the more you want something, the greater risk there is that you will fool yourself into thinking that what you want is what God wants.

I belong to what some would call the "Charismatic stream" of Christianity. My problem is that I don't wade too deep into that stream. You see, I'm a poor excuse for a Charismatic. There are things I care more about than tongues, prophecy, casting out demons, physical healing, etc. I believe in all those things, but I'm more interested in other things. I'm not going to tell you what those other things are because as soon as I do some of you will set me straight saying, "Hey…not fair. I believe in all those things, and I'm a Charismatic." I believe you, I really do.

But I start with Charismatics because we believe God can speak directly to us, kind of like whispering in our ear. Not an audible voice, although many would claim this, and I'm not going to challenge their experience, but an inner voice, a thought that pops into our mind. It's pretty much the same as how other thoughts come to us, but with these thoughts, we have the conviction that they are from God. So we say, "God told me…" or, "Jesus said to me…"

I'm probably overly concerned that my membership in the Charismatic-club might be revoked, so I want to say again that I believe this way of communication can happen, but with this belief comes a certain risk. The risk is that we can mistake what we want for what God wants, or confuse getting an answer to prayer (or a "word from God" as we Charismatics like to say) that agrees with our real, deep down desire for what God said, or didn't say.

This isn't just a weakness with Charismatic theology. One could be a Cessationist and fall into the same error. You might believe that God only speaks today through the Bible. You might want a new car and turn to your Bible for guidance. You flip through the pages and randomly let your eyes fall where they may.

"…and with one accord they came to him…" (Acts 12:20)

There you have it! Off to the Honda dealership.

Sorry.

The point is, whichever stream you're standing in, never underestimate your ability to mistake what you want for what God wants. What you're sensing might be wishful thinking, your imagination, poor hermeneutics, or…it could be God.

Here are four suggestions for limiting the likelihood of mistaking what you want for what God wants.

1. Be self-aware. Are you able to recognize or admit that if it were up to you, you'd choose this or that?

2. Pray honest prayers, something like, "Father, you know that deep down I want to buy a new car, but if this is not your will for me, please help me to see it."

3. _Get a second opinion._ Is there anyone in your life that you can be honest with and who can be honest with you? Your best friend may or may not be the best choice.

"Dude, cool. Let's both go down to the Honda dealership."

4. _Wait before acting._ A good rule to live by, especially when it comes to decision-making is, <u>if you can wait, wait</u>. There has been more than one time that I have wanted to buy something or do something, but while waiting, I discovered that it was not the right thing to do.

<u>Never underestimate your ability to mistake what you want, for what God wants.</u>

57

HOW TO EVALUATE
RECENT EVENTS

Have you ever planned something (an event of some sort, the Sunday morning service, an outreach in your community, a sermon, etc.) and everything worked perfectly?

When a plan works, it really feels good. There are three essentials for pulling off a successful event.

> You plan.
> You execute.
> You evaluate.

I want to focus on the last of these three, evaluate.

Let me share with you four evaluation questions for you and your ministry team to ask following every event. These questions aren't just for pastors. If you lead a team in your church, these four questions can really be helpful.

Let's use the example of the Sunday morning service. Here are four simple questions to ask that will help the Sunday morning experience get better and better. These are helpful questions to ask your staff, your leadership team, your church board, or just you and your spouse.

1. What went right?
2. What went wrong?
3. I there anything that needs to be addressed before next Sunday?
4. What might have been confusing to our guests?

Don't put all your focus on planning and forget the importance of evaluating.

58

HOW TO START OVER

If you could start over, what would you do differently? Now here's my second question: What's preventing you from starting over?

There are probably many things preventing you from starting over, but for now, let's play the 'Starting Over' game.

Here are five steps for starting over:

1. Draw up a list of what you would do differently.
2. Rate the things on your list: 1 = easy to start over and do differently, 2 = hard to start over and do differently, but not impossible, 3 = seemingly impossible to start over, and do differently.
3. Develop a plan for your #1s.

4. Develop a long-term strategy for your #2s. Remember, #2s will be hard but not impossible. Starting over on #2s will take time.
5. Pray over and wait on your #3s.

Does starting over seem a little more realistic now? I hope so. Why not give it a try?

59

HOW TO ASK THE RIGHT QUESTIONS BEFORE PLACING SOMEONE IN LEADERSHIP

1. Do they buy into your values?

Remember that you are the leader; they need to follow your lead, not the other way around. Occasionally someone will join your church with a hidden agenda. As the pastor of the church, you need a leadership team that will support your agenda. For example, if you value being an outward focused church, it will be difficult to do so if one of your leaders does not share that value.

2. Does your spouse feel good about this person?

Now your spouse might be a man, but often I have found women have better discernment than men do about these things. I'm not sure why this seems so, but it has been my experience.

3. Do they seem humble and willing to support your vision? See point #1.

4. Do they come with a good reputation from their previous church? You'll only know if you call their former pastor.

5. Do you like them? I don't think your leaders have to be in your circle of friends, but you need to enjoy them enough to hang out with them once in a while.

6. Do they share your theological convictions? Example: if you believe that women can be pastors and they don't, you're going to have trouble down the road.

The bottom line in selecting leaders is to always choose character over talent and ability. The problem with this is that it takes time to recognize godly character. But your only other option is to haphazardly put people in leadership and hope for the best. Yikes! Remember…it's easier to get them in, than it is to get them out.

60

HOW TO KNOW IF YOUR GREAT IDEA IS FROM GOD

Pastors are always getting inspiration. Sometimes these 'eureka moments' are from God and sometimes not. Just because an idea is not from God doesn't mean it's a bad idea. Non-Christians come up with good ideas all the time.

But the thing is, most pastors barely have enough time to do the things God has clearly asked them to do, so they certainly don't have time to do the things God hasn't asked them to do. How then does one know if their 'great idea' is from God or not?

Ideas that have their origins from God tend to haunt us like Dickens' three spirits. If you forget the idea, there's a good chance it was not God's idea. Ideas that have their origins from our imagination tend to shrink over time. Ideas that have their origins from God tend to grow over time.

Since this is true, we would do well to let our ideas sit for a while. Don't rush the implementation of your inspiration. Put your idea on a shelf for a few days or weeks. Most ideas can wait. If your idea whistles at you every time you walk past that shelf, it might be from God. But remember, that whistling sound might just be an inner-ear problem, so get a second or third opinion.

Ask someone what they think of that light bulb over your head without suggesting that God put it there. When we say to people, "I think God is telling me...", we intimidate and close down feedback we might need to hear.

I know you think your idea is from God, but you might be wrong.

61

HOW TO PREDICT THE FUTURE

Leaders anticipate.

Here are two simple questions you can ask that will help you anticipate future challenges for your church or personal life. You can sit down with your leaders for #1 and with yourself for #2.

1. What do we predict will be the top three challenges our church will face over the next eight months?
2. What do I predict will be the top three challenges I will face over the next eight months?

Ask great questions, and you get great answers.

62

HOW TO KNOW IF IT'S TIME TO CLOSE YOUR CHURCH DOWN

It might surprise you to hear me say this, but sometimes the best thing a pastor can do is close their church down. I should know, I did it once.

I believe that it is hard to kill a church. I've known many that were on the brink of death but then came back to life. However, the smaller the church is, the more fragile it is, and the easier it is to reach a place where it lacks viability.

To determine viability, a church needs to answer these four questions:

1. **Do you have enough money?** If there is not enough money coming in to cover the basic operating expenses of the church (including a livable salary for the pastor, unless he/she is bivocational), then the church is in trouble.

2. **Do you have enough people?** Are there enough active members to cover the most basic ministries and programs one would expect to find in a small church?

3. **Do your people have enough morale and motivation?** You might have enough warm bodies, but if those people are worn out, beaten down, or lack morale and motivation to be about the hard work of turning a church around, the church is in trouble.

4. **Does the pastor have enough energy and motivation to keep going if nothing changes?** A common question I ask pastors is, "How long can you hang in there if nothing changes?" The answer they give tell me a lot about their energy and motivation levels.

Some pastors simply need to take a break. Other pastors need to move on to a new assignment. And some need to quit altogether because the burnout is so great that remaining in the pastorate is not in the best interest of their family or themselves. This last one is really hard for most pastors to admit but it's essential that they do if they really need to.

There is no shame in admitting that your church is no longer viable. There is no shame in admitting that you need to take a break, or move on to a new assignment...or quit.

63

HOW TO KNOW IF YOUR CHURCH NEEDS TO BE BULLDOZED, REMODELED, OR REDECORATED

Sometimes a church needs to be bulldozed or closed down. I've known a couple churches that were so dysfunctional and toxic, that the best thing that could be done for the people, their pastor, and the kingdom of God, would be for them to close their doors.

It's easy, particularly during really difficult times, for the pastor to think that the church is completely broken, and therefore, should be plowed up and started over again. This is usually an exaggeration, and one born out of pain and frustration. One must remember, "It's never completely broken, and it's never completely fixed."

Whenever one is evaluating a church that needs change, or maybe even a ministry department within the church that needs change, the first question that must be asked is: Do we need to bulldoze it, remodel it, or merely redecorate it? What can be left alone and what needs to be changed? And of those things that need to be changed, what can be tweaked, and what needs to be recreated from scratch?

There's seldom a need to tear the whole thing down. Often a church, or ministry department, needs either a remodeling or a redecorating. It is the wise leader who can discern which of the three is needed.

Most churches, even those that are in desperate need of change, have the basics already in place. When this is true, the need is to learn how to do the basics better and more effective. And this always falls into the category of either remodeling or redecorating.

It's one thing to put on a new coat of paint, another thing to tear down a wall, and completely different thing to bring in a bulldozer and level the whole thing.

Remember, it's never completely broken, and it's never completely fixed.

CHURCH HEALTH

64

HOW TO HAVE AN EFFECTIVE SMALL CHURCH

S maller churches lack the resources of larger churches. This does not mean they will not be able to provide meaningful ministry to their members and community, but it does mean they will have to be more selective in what they offer.

In 1948 the first In-N-Out Burger was founded by Harry and Esther Snyder in Baldwin Park, California. Harry's idea of a drive-thru hamburger stand where customers could order through a two-way speaker box was unique. In that era, it was common to see car hops serving those who wanted to order food from their car. Harry's idea caught on, and California's first drive-thru hamburger stand was born.

The Snyder's business philosophy was simple: "Give customers the freshest, highest quality foods you can buy and provide them with friendly service in a sparkling clean environment." These principles have worked so well over the years that they are still the company's fundamental philosophy.

In-N-Out Burger has three items on their menus: burgers, fries, and drinks. There are no salads, no burritos, no chicken sandwiches. Think of the huge variety most other fast food chains offer. You would think In-N-Out made a mistake in limiting what they offer, but they continue to be one of the most popular food chains in California, Nevada, and Arizona.

I think smaller churches need to follow the example of In-N-Out...do a few things well and, "Give customers the freshest, highest quality foods you can buy and provide them with friendly service in a sparkling clean environment."

What do you have the resources to do? By adding more ministries prematurely are you running the risk of providing a poor product, and equally as bad, burned out workers? It would be better to do a few things well than a bunch of things half-baked that wear your volunteers out.

> If you can't do multimedia well, don't do multi-media.
> If you don't have the human resources to do a full-on children's ministry program, don't do one.

> If there are no resources and interest
> for doing small groups, let it go and wait
> until the time is right.

You get the point.

Smaller churches need to copy In-N-Out, not Denny's. Denny's offers everything you could ever want. In-N-Out...burgers, fries, and drinks. Since mission statements are so popular these days, perhaps your mission statement should be In-N-Out's: "Give customers the freshest, highest quality foods you can buy and provide them with friendly service in a sparkling clean environment."

65

HOW TO ESTABLISH AND MAINTAIN THE PRIORITIES OF YOUR CHURCH

We tend to drift away from, rather than towards, the priorities of our church. Like a riptide that pulls us from shore, there are forces at play that pull us from the things that we value, from the primary, from our goals.

Do you have 'established' priorities? The word 'establish' comes from the Latin and means 'to make firm.' Are your priorities firm, are they written down? Could you easily recite your values or the values of your church? Could your leadership team quote the priorities/values of your church? If you or they can't, then your priorities are probably not established.

One of the more common problems I run into with pastors and churches is a lack of focus and a failure to establish priorities. The pastor, or the church they lead, fluctuates from one focus to the next with no rhyme or reason.

The first challenge is to identify and establish the priorities of your church. Prayerfully sit with a yellow-pad, or your laptop, and invite the Holy Spirit to come and show you what your priorities are, or should be. Write them down. Establish them. Make them firm.

After this, the next step, the one that is equally as challenging, is to focus on your priorities/values, and never stop. By 'focusing' on your priorities, I'm referring to the means by which you will demonstrate or express your priorities. The expression of priorities can change, but your priorities, or values, seldom change.

> Identify, focus, establish, maintain.
> Identify, focus, establish, maintain.

One of the most common challenges pastors face is the constant challenge of establishing and maintaining church priorities and values.

How is this going for you?

66

HOW TO RECOGNIZE AND REJECT A CULTURALLY IMPOSED DEFINITION OF SUCCESS

The church in America defines success almost exclusively by numbers, i.e., how many were in attendance, and how much was in the offering?

There were times when I didn't look forward to hanging out with pastors because I knew that eventually, someone was going to ask me, "So...how are things going at your church?" This question is usually the way one pastor finds out if they are more or less successful than another pastor.

If my church was growing (which was seldom) then I didn't mind answering their question. If my church was not growing (which was often), I asked to be excused, said something about the stomach flu, and ran out the door.

Seriously, it didn't matter how many good things were happening in my church; I didn't feel successful if my church was in decline or had plateaued for a long period. Someone could have been raised from the dead, and I'd be thinking, "That's nice, but that church down the street, the one that is bigger than us, they're more successful than we are."

I like to challenge pastors to sit down with their leaders and discover ways to define success in their church that have very little to do with size or numbers.

There's a difference between wanting to have success and needing to have success in order to feel good about yourself and your church. We need to detach from the need to be thought of as successful.

Rather than asking questions like, "How large is my church?", try answering questions such as:

> Am I faithful to my family?
> Am I faithful to my call?
> Is my church healthy?
> How will I determine if my church is healthy?
> What percentage of my church is involved in a ministry?
> Do my people seem to be growing in their relationship with Jesus?
> Is there joy when my people gather?
> Are my people inviting new people to church or other related events?

What are we doing to reach new people?
Are my people generous with their time,
money, and gifts?

Can you think of any other questions?

I know you've been told, "All healthy things grow and reproduce.", but this isn't always true. I work with many healthy churches that are small, are not growing, or have plateaued. My experience has been that you can have a healthy church that isn't growing and you can have an unhealthy church that is growing.

When you talk to pastors in countries that have not been affected by our American brand of Christianity, you soon discover that they are not as concerned with numbers as we are.

It's important that we are able to recognize what are culturally imposed expectations for us as pastors and for our churches, and what are Biblically imposed expectations. These can be, and often are, different.

67

HOW TO LEARN FROM THE DIET INDUSTRY ABOUT CHURCH HEALTH

Several years ago I went on one of those low-carb diets. In about nine months I lost 40 pounds! I managed to stay at my dream weight for about two days. A year later my weight was back to where I started. I had never before jumped on one of those diet bandwagons, but low-carb was in, and I fell for it.

Over the years there have been many fad diets. In the 70's, diet pills were popular. In the 80's there was the Scarsdale Diet, then came Atkins in the 90's. Today some of the most popular diets are celebrity-endorsed diets. Jennifer Aniston (from the hit comedy series FRIENDS) was into The Zone. The Kardashians, QuickTrim. Beyonce promoted (and I don't even want to know what this involves) the Master Cleanse.

Diet fads come and go, but the nutrition experts keep saying the same thing: "Diets don't work! Watch your portions. Get some exercise. Eat fewer calories than you burn. Lose weight slowly, and you'll probably keep it off. You've got to change your life-style."

In other words, focus on the basics.

There's always going to be a new diet that promises results. And there are always going to be new ways to do church that promise results also. Some of these models work for some and not for others. Some fade away never to be heard from again.

We've been told to have a small group focused church, a seeker-sensitive church, a postmodern church. I can't figure out if my problem is that I'm not Missional enough or not Emergent enough. I hear the Attractional model is dead. Should I have a cell church, house church, or simple church? I just read an article telling me that Evangelicalism is on the way out, so I need to find what's on the way in and join them.

The above models, those that have passed and those that are current, all have something legitimate to say. But it seems to me that we need to simply focus on the old tried and true basics: eat fewer calories than you burn, get some exercise, more fruits and vegetables, and give it time. Get it?

Why not take a moment to reflect on the following two questions: 1) What are some of the church-basics? 2) How well am I doing with those basics?

68

HOW TO MEASURE
CHURCH HEALTH

I have to admit that there does seem to be more talk these days about church health along with church growth. However, sometimes church health is secretly the focus one employs to achieve what they are really after...Church growth. The easy way to spot this is if you hear the person promoting church health make some comment like, "Church health will lead to church growth. A healthy church will be a growing church." Sometimes this is true, but not always. You can have a healthy church that is not growing, and you can have a growing church that is not healthy. Numbers are not necessarily an indication of health or lack thereof. How then can we measure church health?

Percentages.

A church is healthy if there is a growing percentage of its members involved in things like small groups, serving in ministries, personal evangelism, personal devotions, tithing, etc. For example, a church with an attendance of 100 that has 35% of its members participating in outreach activities would be healthier (at least in the area of outreach) than a church of 1000 that only has 20% involvement. A church of 200 with 40% involvement in small groups and a church of 3000 with 40% involvement would be equally healthy in the area of small groups.

The Pareto Principle

The Pareto principle (also known as the 80-20 rule, or the law of the vital few and the principle of factor sparseness) states that, for many phenomena, 80% of the consequences stem from 20% of the causes. Business management thinker Joseph M. Juran suggested the principle and named it after Italian economist Vilfredo Pareto, who observed that 80% of income in Italy went to 20% of the population. It is a common rule of thumb in business; e.g., 80% of your sales come from 20% of your clients.

If the Pareto principle is true in business, it is certainly true in most churches. Doesn't it seem like 80% of your giving comes from 20% of your people? Don't 20% of your people do 80% of the work? Therefore, 20% involvement in personal devotions would be

normal (not necessarily good, but normal) and anything above that is movement up the church health
scale.

Leadership Team Project:

Want an interesting and helpful activity for you and
your leaders? At your next leadership team meeting:

1. Draw up a list of things you would hope your
   members would participate in, things that you
   think are healthy for Christians, i.e., small
   groups, serving in ministries, etc.
2. Figure out what percentage of your adult members are participating in each of the areas you
   identified.
3. Determine a way to track these percentages so
   that six months from now you can see if the
   percentages have grown, remained the same,
   or declined.
4. Score each area based on the Pareto principle.
   Below 20% is below normal. 20% is normal.
   Above 20% is better than normal. The higher
   the percentage, the higher degree of health.

Sometimes smaller churches are healthier than they realize. We must discover ways to determine health, ways
other than merely looking at attendance. 'Percentages'
is an objective and accurate way to measure the health
of your church.

69

HOW TO CREATE OWNERSHIP
IN YOUR CHURCH

Have you ever had a great idea, I mean, really felt God was leading you into some focus or direction for the church, but when it came time to communicate it to your congregation they just stared at you like zombies? Or maybe you had coffee with someone in your church because you think they'd be great at heading up some ministry. You lay out the need, explain the commitment, and are overjoyed to hear them say, "Well Pastor, if you think I'd be good at it I'll give it a try." You skip away congratulating yourself on what an awesome recruiter you are. But then it happens, it might take a couple of months, but it happens, they resign or end up needing so much hand-holding that you regret ever giving them the responsibility in the first place.

With both scenarios, chances are your people didn't have ownership.

Ownership is when your people are as sold on and excited about an idea or project as you are...or at least pretty close. Ownership is important. Remember this rule: No ownership = zombies. And don't forget, zombies, with very few exceptions, make poor parishioners.

There are four steps to building ownership.

Step One: Be open to the fact that not all good ideas will originate with you or be carried out based on your conviction and enthusiasm alone.

Step Two: Be inclusive. Include people in the decision-making process. If people feel like they've been included, it is more likely they will feel they have ownership.

Step Three: Be willing to risk. If you include people in the decision-making process you can bet they will come up with ideas you never thought of, many of them will be good ideas, and some of them poor ideas. The temptation with poor ideas is for the pastor to quickly shoot them down. Usually it's better to let someone try their idea and discover for themselves that it didn't work, than to see you close the door on it before they had a chance to try.

Step Four: Be patient. It takes time to create ownership. Chances are that your good idea is something you've been kicking around in your mind for some time. Give your people the same time to think, digest, object, brainstorm, and pray. This might mean your implementation will be slower, but in the end, it will be more solid.

And remember...Jesus loves your zombies.

70

HOW TO AVOID INSANITY
IN YOUR CHURCH

Your church is perfectly designed to get the re-sults it's currently getting. If you want something different, you'll probably need to do something different. Albert Einstein is reported to have said, "Insanity is doing the same thing over and over again and expecting different results."

I'm sorry to say this, but there are a lot of insane small churches out there, and, to be fair, there are a lot of insane large churches out there. There are a lot of insane small church pastors and insane large church pastors. There are a lot of insane small church boards/leaders, and there are a lot of insane church boards/leaders of large churches. There's a lot of insanity happening out there in our churches.

There are three types of churches: those that are growing, those that have plateaued, and those in decline. Regardless of what we've been told, there are no simple answers for why one church grows over another. There are no simple answers for why a church has plateaued. There are no simple answers for why a church is experiencing decline. Anyone who offers simplistic answers to these dynamics is being...well, simplistic, maybe even naive.

Just because a church is growing is no guarantee that the church is healthy. Just because a church has plateaued is no guarantee that the church is unhealthy. Sometimes (not very often but sometimes) a church can be in decline, and be healthy.

Again, your church is perfectly designed to get the results it's currently getting. If you want something different, you'll probably need to do something different.

If your church is growing, you might be pleased with your results, but if your church has plateaued or is in decline, you probably are not pleased. If you want something different you'll need to do something different, and the change needed to turn things around might be significant.

Herein lies the greatest challenge we face when trying to move our congregations in a new or different direction...people don't want to change.

People want to keep doing what they've always done. People might be interested in change as long as you're not asking them to change something that is important to them.

"And no one after drinking the old wine wants the new, for he says, 'The old is better.'" (Luke 5:39)

It is so common for pastors, or congregants, or church boards, to want their church to grow but are reluctant (or down right resistant) to embrace the significant change that is often required to bring about the change. Doing the same things but expecting different outcomes is insanity.

If you pastor a church that has been plateaued for the past three years or has been in decline for the past three years, I suggest the following steps:

1. Form a team of 'prayers' who see what you see and feel what you feel. Begin to pray for guidance from God as to what you should or could do.

2. Begin the process of re-educating your church in regards to the dynamics of change. Don't begin by listing all the areas that need to change; this will probably scare many of your people away. Start with your board or key leaders. Teach on the topic of change. Once you feel that your most influential people are on board, begin to re-educate your congregation about the importance of embracing change.

3. Be patient. Selling 'change' takes time. Never underestimate how much 'change' freaks people out. Take things slowly.

4. Form a team of spiritually mature 'thinkers' who will partner with you and prayerfully identify the significant areas that will need to change for your church to turn and go in a new direction.

5. Prayerfully prioritize this list.

6. Begin at the top and slowly work your way down.

Don't settle for an insane church.

71

HOW TO GO FROM A 'CHURCH GROWTH' TO A 'CHURCH HEALTH' FOCUS

There is a difference between church growth and church health. I believe you can have church health without church growth and church growth without church health.

The Church Growth Movement experts told us, "All healthy things grow and reproduce." But that's not always true. I'm healthy, but I'm no longer physically growing. A woman can be passed the age to conceive, but we would not say because of this she is not healthy. It's not that there isn't any truth to, "All healthy things grow and reproduce.", it's just that it's not always true. And, when you apply this to church growth, i.e., "Since all healthy things grow and reproduce, then healthy churches will grow and reproduce.", you begin to get into trouble; the saying begins to break down.

I've been coaching pastors and consulting churches for more than ten years now. Some of my clients
have healthy churches that are not growing, and some
of them have unhealthy churches that are not growing. And don't get me started with the strange phenomenon that occurs occasionally when you have an
unhealthy church that is growing.

At the beginning of any coaching relationship,
I make sure the pastor understands that I am not a
'church growth' guy, but that I'm a 'church health'
guy. I explain to them that one of the things I'm good
at is helping pastors and their leaders identify saboteurs of growth.

There are things we can be doing, or things we're
not doing that can sabotage growth. In other words,
it's hard enough to grow a church, let's not help the
'hard' out. I make clear to the pastor, however, that
we can identify saboteurs of growth, correct them, and
there still is no guarantee that the church will grow.

So then, why bother?

We bother because we want to have a healthy
church whether it's large or small. And certainly, no
one argues that an unhealthy church is unlikely to become a growing church. At the same time, we do not
want to use "church health" as just another gimmick
that we hope, or assume, will result in church growth.

Think of church health as water hold up behind a
dam. The water is there; all you need do is blow up the
dam. Sit down with your leaders and kick around the

question, "What might there be in our church that is damming up the water? What might be blocking the flow of health or growth?" Or, lead your team into a discussion of, "Are there things we're doing or not doing that might be sabotaging church health or church growth?"

Come up with your list of saboteurs. Prioritize your list and start working on improving those things. Maybe you don't have enough dynamite to blow up the dam. Maybe all you can do is chip away at it a little at a time. Any movement, no matter how small, that takes you towards health rather than away from health, is good.

72

HOW TO KEEP YOUR CHURCH MOVING FORWARD

Remember Newton's first two laws of motion? Here's a refresher.

First law: Every object continues in its state of rest, or of uniform motion in a straight line, unless compelled to change that state by external forces acted upon it.

Second law: The acceleration of a body is parallel and directly proportional to the net force acting on the body, is in the direction of the net force, and is inversely proportional to the mass of the body.

In other words, things that are aren't moving don't move unless something pushes them, pulls them, or otherwise compels them by force, and this includes churches.

If you are a pastor, begin by asking yourself the following question and then share the question with your leadership team.

What will we need to do differently in the next twelve months to see something different than what we saw in the previous twelve months?

73

HOW TO FIGURE OUT WHO, OR WHAT, IS TO BLAME FOR YOUR LACK OF GROWTH

In Mark 4 we have the very familiar parable, The Sower And The Seed. In this story we have the man, the seed, and the soil. The seed is symbolic of the Gospel or God's word. When I think of a church that is not producing a crop, it seems the only possibilities for blame are either the man (the pastor) or the soil (the people making up the congregation, or possibly, the community the pastor is trying to reach).

Some pastors I talk to have very poor soil to work with. Occasionally I run into poor pastors, by this I mean, poor in the sense that their gifting, skills, training, and temperament are such that they are not what they could be or should be to effectively lead a church, but this is rare.

The seed (the Gospel/God's word) is completely reliable. There is never a problem with the seed.

I often think that some churches will never be healthy and happy. I have more hope for the "poor pastor" because skills can be learned and personality can be worked around. But if you have poor soil…that's a hard one.

When a pastor has good soil, the crops come much easier than the pastor who has poor soil. When you bring together a poor pastor with poor soil, there is almost no hope unless, of course, there occurs an unsolicited, or solicited, sovereign invasion of Holy Spirit renewal or revival.

If a pastor has poor soil, it is unlikely that anything they try will work or produce a crop. Until the quality of soil improves, he or she will continue to labor in vain. But this is exactly what many pastors do: they ignore the soil and focus on other things, good things, but the 'good things' don't really effect the soil.

Questions for a pastor and leadership team to ask are:

1. Do the ministries in our church result in a higher quality of soil?
2. What does good soil look like?
3. What produces good soil?
4. What is our soil like?
5. What could we do differently to increase the quality of soil?

74

HOW TO INCREASE
WORSHIP-DYNAMIC BY 50%

After you read this you might want to pass it on to your worship leader or music director.

Some people have told me I have a nice singing voice. Actually, I always wanted to be a singer. It all started when I was much younger, and my parents would leave the house. I would get out their Tom Jones albums (It's Not Unusual, What's New Pussycat, Delilah, etc.) grab a spoon for a microphone, and belt one out.

Anyway...I began singing in choir in Jr. High, and then in High School. I had my first duet my freshman year for a Christmas concert singing alongside a senior named Nancy. I can't remember her last name, but I do remember she was pretty and had a beautiful voice. We sat on two stools with an orchestra backing us up and a few hundred people out in the audience. Next,

I landed the role of Conrad Birdie in our high school musical 'Bye, Bye, Birdie.' I had the largest costume budget of anyone in the show. Imagine Elvis performing and then imagine me wearing his on-stage attire. Now pray to God to remove that image from your mind.

At the beginning of my sophomore year, I was asked if I was interested in touring with our school's jazz band the next summer as their crooner. I thought about it for about two seconds and said "yes!" This was going to be my big break. But a few months later, at school, while walking into the music department, (Oh, I forgot to mention that the summer of my sophomore year I became a Christian) I heard a voice say, "You're not going to go into entertainment. You're going to pastor my people." That brought to an end my brief rise to stardom.

One of my first church ministries was leading worship for an evening service at the church I was attending. I must have been seventeen or eighteen. I didn't play an instrument, so I sat on a stool (this time without Nancy next to me) a led a-cappella. A few years later Ellen and I would be church planters in Southern California. There was no one to lead worship, so I taught myself five chords on the guitar and forced every song we sang to fit into those five cords. Luckily the Lord brought me some good musicians and worship leaders who would rescue me, and the church. I led worship for our second church plant. In our third church plant, we were blessed with a great worship leader and band, so my career as a worship leader was over.

I've said all this to show that I have some experience as both a vocalist and a worship leader. Since then, as you can imagine, I've listened to many worship leaders. I've listened to them in churches where I was the guest speaker. I've listened to them on the radio while driving. One night I was watching a station on television that featured worship services from different churches across the nation. And, of course, every Sunday I listen to the talented worship leaders at our home church.

There is a universal problem. I see this problem everywhere. I believe this problem can cause the worship dynamic to drop by 50%.

The one thing worship leaders need to stop doing is (worship drum-roll please) playing songs in keys that most men and women cannot possibly sing in. The songs are just too high for a normal human. The result? People don't sing. The result? Worship dynamic drops.

I have an unusual vocal range for a man. I can sing baritone, and I can sing high tenor. Because of my background in music, I know how to harmonize or drop down into a lower range to sing a song more comfortably, but I still find it a bit distracting when I need to do this. Most people don't know how to do this.

Dear worship leader, might I offer some advice that could increase the dynamic of your worship by 50%? Learn to transpose your songs down into a range that people can comfortably sing in. This is true of hymns as well. Just because a song was written in a certain key does not mean you have to sing it in that key. It seems that many worship songwriters today, with their typical tenor voices, miss this. They can hit those notes, you might be able to hit those notes, but those you are attempting to lead into the presence of God can't hit those notes. People need to be able to sing the songs you've selected for your worship set.

Bottom line: transpose your songs down, and your worship dynamic will go up. Trust me; this comes from a man who learned to sing from Tom Jones.

OUTREACH

75

HOW TO MOTIVATE YOUR PEOPLE TO SHARE THEIR FAITH

A church, left to itself, will not naturally gravitate towards being outward focused. A church, left to itself, naturally gravitates towards being inward focused. It's the job of the pastor not to let the church be left to itself. This can be the hardest job a pastor has. If the pastor values outreach and personal evangelism they will need to pound this value into the hearts and minds of their people.

Here are six steps to motivate your people to share their faith.

Model. The pastor has to model this value. It's great when the pastor has stories to tell of his or her personal experiences in sharing their faith with others. The problem with this is that parishioners expect the pastor to be sharing their faith (that's their job), so testimonies like this have less of an effect than we would hope for.

Define. A while ago George Barna did a study and discovered that an alarmingly high percentage of church goers were unable to define the 'Gospel.' Don't assume your people know what you mean when you use words like: outreach, evangelism, sharing your faith, etc.

Demystify. I believe we need to help people see how evangelism can happen naturally throughout their week. Often when people think of evangelism they think of an 'Evangelist,' or walking up to a complete stranger and telling them about Jesus, or knocking on a stranger's door. Being 'light and salt' should be a lifestyle rather than an event.

Equip. Train your people how to explain the gospel in one to three minutes. Give your people ideas on how to recognize opportunities that present themselves to share their faith. Give them examples of how to initiate a conversation about spiritual things.

Celebrate. As your people begin to step out and share, they will have stories to tell. Give them an opportunity to share these stories on Sunday morning.

Celebrate any opportunity someone had to represent Jesus to someone. Remember the principle: Celebrate what you want to reproduce.

Repeat. This process never ends. You keep doing it and doing it and doing it because a church left to itself naturally gravitates away from, rather than towards, an outward focus.

76

HOW TO REACH NEW PEOPLE

First of all, this could be one of the most important questions for you and your leadership team to ask: What are we doing to reach new people? The second best question is a follow-up to the first: So, how's that working for us?

Have you noticed that evangelism and outreach programs seldom work? And if they do 'work,' the results are way off from what we hoped for. And another thing, if our 'program' actually results in someone talking to a non-Christian and inviting them to church or getting them to accept Jesus, typically we never see them again.

Have you noticed that?

I hope that many of you will write me back objecting and sharing countless stories of how your evangelism and outreach programs worked, still work, and how you couldn't be happier.

However, the absolute best way to reach new people is through renewed people. People, not programs, reach new people.

Every year I keep waiting for a new study that will contradict previous studies telling us that the number one way people come to visit a church is by the invitation of someone they know and trust. I'm waiting for someone to prove that door to door works, that billboards work, that newspaper adds work, a free car wash works, kitten giveaways work. Nope, what do the experts keep telling us? The number one way to get people to visit your church is to inspire your people to invite their friends, relatives, neighbors, and co-workers to church, or a church event.

You reach new people through renewed people. I wonder what would happen if we spent as much money and time and resources on creating 'inviters' as we did on outreach and evangelism events? I think I know what would happen. We would see a consistent flow of guests and visitors.

What are you doing to reach new people?

77

HOW TO HAVE A SUMMER OUTREACH EVENT THAT IS FUN, WORKS, AND TASTY

Summer is a perfect time to begin planning a Barbeque Competition Sunday. We tried this in our last church and it was a big success. And why wouldn't it be, everyone loves barbeque? But this is a barbeque with a good-natured competition and outreach twist.

It's simple, those entering the competition bring their own barbeques with them on Sunday and set up before the service or immediately after. Teams can be formed by families, singles, home groups, etc. The teams supply their own meat, chicken, links, whatever, and the church provides drinks and paper goods.

Remember that this will be lunch for everyone, so you'll need to figure out how much food each team should prepare to ensure there's enough for the whole

DAVE JACOBS

crowd. You might want to have some activity planned for the children to keep them occupied after the service and before the food is served.

Each team will be scored on taste, enthusiasm, and how well their booth is decorated. Here's the great part, you and your board are the judges...yum. To make it even more fun, bribing the judges is encouraged. Trophies can be awarded to the most flavorful, the most enthusiastic, best decorations, and best all around.

This is an easy event for your members to invite their unchurched friends and relatives too. Once again, everyone loves barbeque...especially free barbeque!

78

HOW TO DEVELOP A MORE OUTWARD-FOCUSED CHURCH

I was asked by 200churches.com (a podcast specifically focused on small church ministry) to come up with a list of the top challenges pastors face. One of the top challenges pastors are constantly facing is that of moving their church towards an outward focus.

A church, left alone, will naturally lean towards an inward focus (ministries and programs they have that meet the needs of their current members) rather than an outward focus (ways they are reaching new people).

It's kind of like a fire. Fire, left alone, will eventually cool off rather than heat up. I've never known a church that started out with an outward focus, continue in that direction without a strategic plan and continual push by the pastor and the leaders of the church.

In a sense, it's a little easier for new church plants than it is for already established churches because in a new church the focus, in the beginning, is growing the church. But even in a new church, once they begin to grow, once they start developing some of the more common departments, (Children's ministries, small groups, etc.) slowly…ever so slowly, outreach begins to suffer.

If this is one of your current challenges let me make four suggestions:

1. Do you believe with all your heart that the church exists to reach new people with the good news of Jesus? I know that seems like a stupid question to ask pastors, but you'd be surprised how some need to be reminded of this. I'm not suggesting that the needs of your current people are not important. They are. You can have your cake and eat it too. The challenge for many pastors, however, is that the slice of (inward focus) cake is larger than the slice of (outward focus) cake. Part of this is because our time is often focused on maintaining inward focused stuff in our churches rather than outward focused stuff. The bottom line, if you are not passionate about reaching new people, it is doubtful that your church will be.

2. Do your core leaders, church board, elders, whatever you call them, believe with all their

hearts that the church exists to reach new people with the good news of Jesus? If your answer is 'no' then you will need to begin the process of re-educating them. This will take time. This will probably be met with some resistance. Be patient. The bottom line…if your key leaders are not passionate about reaching new people, it is doubtful that the rest of your church will be.

3. Discover those in your church who are passionate about reaching new people. Get them in a room together for prayer and Spirit-inspired brainstorming.

In this group, questions can be discussed such as:

What percentage of our money and energy are spent on inward focused things rather than outward focused things?

When was the last time we reached, and kept, a new person? How many of our additions are Christians transferring from another church versus adding people previously unchurched?

What different ways might we gradually change our church culture to become more outward focused?

In what ways might our current Sunday morning service seem confusing, uncomfortable, or strange to an unchurched person?

The following question is particularly helpful if your church is primarily made up of elderly Christians:

If we don't reach new, younger people, how long before we die out?

4. Gather a small group (even if it's only you and your spouse) and begin praying, "Father, help us to have a greater outward focus. Father, we know you love lost people. Forgive us for being so inward focused. Show us Father, how we might get better at reaching new people. We anticipate some resistance, possibly even from some of our members, and ask that you would go before us. Father, give us the lost!"

79

HOW TO MOVE FROM EVANGELISTIC PROGRAMS TO INVITERS AND INCLUDERS

There's a lot of talk these days about taking the church to the unchurched (Missional) instead of expecting the unchurched to come to church (Attractional). I understand what's behind this, but does it have to be either/or? We desire to see our members walking out their faith where they live and work and play. We want them to "be the church, not merely go to church." Also, we don't want our people to abdicate their responsibility to share their faith by relying on their pastor to do it for them on Sunday morning. Fair enough, but I still believe that inviting a friend to church is a legitimate example of personal evangelism.

People continue to respond to invitations to come to church. I've read that 63% would respond favorably to an invitation from a friend or neighbor to come to church. Chances are the majority of the members of your church are there because someone invited them, they came, they liked it, and they stayed. In addition to this, a large percentage of believers say they became Christians by responding to the gospel message or an invitation made to receive Christ in church. There's nothing wrong with training your people to be inviters and includers with a specific emphasis on inviting their friends, relatives, neighbors, and co-workers to church.

Inviting someone to church is not the only way to do personal evangelism, but it is a way. If you are going to create inviters and includers then you'll need to do eight things:

1. You have to model it. When was the last time you invited someone to church? Remember, you reproduce what you are.

2. You have to pound the concept into them and alter their mental DNA. You have to talk about being inviters and includers over and over and over again.

3. You have to provide something relevant and safe for them to invite people to. Somehow discover a way to objectively determine if your Sunday morning service feels relevant and safe to visitors. Relevance can be achieved without compromise.

4. You have to celebrate victories. Remember, every time someone invites someone to church it is a victory regardless if the one invited comes or not.

5. You have to be committed to this for the long haul. Altering the DNA of your people, creating inviters and includers, takes time.

6. You must not be afraid to present the gospel sometime during your service. Develop a streamlined version of the plan of salvation that you can share in two minutes or less. One advantage of sharing the gospel on Sunday mornings is that your regulars end up learning what the gospel message is.

7. You must not be afraid to ask for a decision. It doesn't matter if you ask for a show of hands, or to sign a card, or come forward, or whatever...what matters is that you give visitors an opportunity to respond. I know that raising one's hand is no guarantee the person has truly been converted, but leave that to God.

8. You must have a plan for follow-up. Somehow, someway you need to have a way to make contact with those who visit your church or make a decision for Christ. It's always amazing to me when I hear of a church that has no follow-up plan. Remember, Jesus said, "You have not because you follow up not." No, not really.

80

HOW TO KNOW WHAT GUESTS ARE REALLY THINKING

If you're a pastor, it's probably been a while since you've been a visitor in someone else's church. I mean a visitor in the sense of one looking for a new church home. After Ellen and I moved to Southern Oregon, it took us a couple of months to decide on a church to join. Moving put us in that unfamiliar place of looking for a church. Just think, for twenty-eight years I'd never gone church shopping. Ellen and I have always started our own churches and had people visit us, not the other way around. It's a very interesting experience, i.e., looking at a church through the eyes of a visitor.

They say that first-time visitors decide if they are going to return to your church a second time within the first seven minutes they walk through your doors. Even if this were nothing more than a 'church' urban legend, I would probably agree...give or take a few minutes.

The point is, you will become blind to how your church looks to first-timers in direct proportion to how old your church is and how long you have been there. The longer you've been 'open for business', the less likely it is that you can tell what comes off as strange, confusing, or weird to those who are visiting. To remedy this, you might need to **plant a spy.** There are two ways you might do this.

First, find someone in your church you feel can be truly objective and understands what it is you are trying to accomplish. The following Sunday, have them come a few minutes late and take notes of everything that stands out to them that might be a turn-off to a guest. Their challenge is to see your service through the eyes of a guest, whether they are a Christian guest looking for a new church home, or an unbeliever checking your church out for whatever reason.

Or...

Second, and this is probably the best way to get some truly unbiased feedback, pay some unchurched non-believer to help you out. Have them visit your church, fill out a questionnaire, and meet with you afterward for a debriefing. Pay them $25 – $50. It will be worth it.

If we want to attract the unchurched, we must learn to see our meetings through their eyes. An attempt needs to be made to remove any obstacles that might keep them from returning, within reason of course. One of the best ways of identifying and removing said obstacles is to plant a spy.

81

HOW TO HAVE
A CARE-PACKAGE SUNDAY

Want to have an outreach project that everyone in your church will participate in? Want to have an outreach project that is fun and will cost you next to nothing? Want to have an outreach project that will produce great stories for your congregation to tell? If so, why not try a Care Package Sunday.

How many times have members of your church told you about some homeless person either coming up to them asking for money or advertising their need for it at an intersection, and your church member doesn't know what to do? They don't want to give them cash for fear that they will use it for alcohol or drugs (which is an assumption on their part), but they wish they could do something.

A 'care package' is a plastic bag filled with non-perishable goods like granola bars, socks, soap, pop-top fruit cans, tooth paste, tooth brush, etc., that church members can keep with them in the back seat of their cars. When they come upon a homeless person, they have something to give them.

A Care Package Sunday is a Sunday morning dedicated solely to the assembly of these care packages. In my former church, we did this once a year for a number of years. It was one of the most anticipated Sundays of the year. Here's how it looked:

The people would arrive with all the articles for the care packages all lined up in front the auditorium. Think of an assembly line. These articles had been donated by local businesses. Usually, this outreach never cost us a dime. We would have a shorter worship time. I would speak for about ten minutes on the subject of showing mercy to those in need.

The rest of the meeting consisted of the people getting in line to assemble their care packages. If there are enough supplies then people could get back in line and assemble another bag. When there were no supplies left we would reassemble and pray that God would bring to us those who needed these bags. Then we would worship and go home.

For the following few Sundays I'd ask if there was anyone who had an opportunity to give away a bag and if they would like to share the experience with the congregation. It was so exciting to hear the stories.

PREACHING

82

HOW TO TEACH ON TITHING

Recently, on my Small Church Pastor group page on Facebook, I posted, "We have this idea that if you teach on tithing, you'll get tithers. When has that ever really happened?"

Before I get to my first reason why teaching on tithing doesn't work, let's remember that Christians can read the same Bible and come to different conclusions about tithing. Some believe that the Bible teaches tithing for Christians today and some disagree. Same Bible, but different conclusions. Both love the word of God, but both have different positions on this. So, if you don't teach tithing then simply substitute 'giving' or 'stewardship' and this will still relate. Having said that...

The first reason why teaching on tithing doesn't work is that we don't teach on tithing very often. We've been told that one reason why people don't like churches is because, 'They're always talking about money.' I'm sure there are plenty of those churches out there, but usually when I am talking to a pastor they confess that they don't like to talk about money, or tithing, and therefore, don't do so as often as they think they should.

> Pastor Bill: Dave, our giving is down. I don't know what to do. Can we talk about that?
> Me: Sure. Is this a three-month or a six-month trend, or something that has been happening for a few weeks or maybe a month?
> Pastor Bill: This started the end of last year and has continued to today.
> Me: When was the last time you taught on tithing or giving?
> Pastor Bill: Oh...let me think about that...Um...it's been a while.

If you believe in tithing (or stewardship, or whatever word best describes what you think the Bible has to say about giving) but seldom teach on it, how do you expect one sermon a year to do the trick? If tithing (or stewardship, or whatever word best describes what you think the Bible has to say about giving) is such a big deal, then why do we teach on it so infrequently? I think one reason is, possibly the number one reason is...fear.

We're afraid that visitors will lump us in with the television preachers who are constantly asking for money. We're afraid that we might offend members of our church who in turn might leave or cause trouble for us. These are legitimate fears. I don't fault a pastor for worrying about this. Remember, I was a pastor for twenty-eight years. I know these fears.

Jesus talked a lot about money, material possessions, and our attitudes and practices concerning them. Don't be afraid to talk about tithing or stewardship, but do so without coming across heavy-handed, or resorting to guilt and shame. Have you noticed that guilt and shame seldom motivate people to change?

The third reason why preaching on tithing doesn't work it because we wait until the church is in trouble financially or until we're mad. Often these go hand in hand.

Not too long ago I was talking to a pastor who was concerned about a downward trend in giving in his church. The pastor was facing the very real possibility of taking a cut in pay. His family was already barely getting by. I could tell he was frustrated (who wouldn't be?), and I could tell he was mad. He wanted to discuss the need to preach on tithing. But before we went any further, the conversation went something like this:

> Me: You sound pretty mad.
> Bill (not his real name): I don't mean
> to sound that way. I'm not mad; it's just

frustrating to hear how people spend their money with no regard to the church or tithing.

Me: I get that...but you sound pretty angry.

Bill (short pause): Well, I guess you're right. I am mad.

Me: I understand. But you might want to deal with those feelings before you preach a sermon on tithing or address this problem to the church.

If we are angry, that vibe will slip out no matter how good we think we are at hiding our true feelings. Anger, irritation, guilt or shame, are poor motivators. Always deal with your frustration or anger before you preach, and especially if you're planning to preach on tithing.

The fourth reason why preaching on tithing doesn't work is because it doesn't work, at least not to the degree we hoped it would.

On my group page I was surprised by how many (actually only a few, but still) reported that they had pretty good luck with preaching on tithing. Usually, for me, when talking to a pastor about this, the conversation goes something like...

Pastor Bill: I'm really concerned about our giving. If something doesn't change, we're going to be in trouble soon.

> Me: How do you intend to respond to
> this?
> Pastor Bill: Well it's been a while since
> I've taught on tithing. I guess it's time.
> Me: How did it go the last time you
> preached on tithing?
> Pastor Bill: Well, giving went up a little
> but then it crept back down.
> Me: What are your reasons for believing
> that you will get different results this
> time?

When we talk about teaching on tithing 'working,'
I'm assuming we mean it results in people who were
not tithing, changing and becoming tithers, perma-
nent tithers. And what we're hoping for is that a large
enough group of non-tithers will become tithers so
that it will turn things around for us as a church financially, especially if we are barely getting by or are in
financial trouble.

There is an explanation why preaching on tithing
seldom gives us the results we're looking for.

We have this idea that if people don't tithe, we can
correct this by teaching on tithing. The assumptions
are, a) they don't know about tithing and once they
hear about it they will change, b) they know about
tithing but have drifted out of the habit of tithing
and once we teach about it they will change, c) they
know perfectly well about tithing but are ignoring the

scriptures, and once we teach about it they will come under conviction, run forward during your sermon weeping and wailing and begging you to take their money.

I don't doubt that sometimes one of these three happen, but this is rare.

Here is the fifth reason why preaching on tithing doesn't work. I think we miss the underlying reasons why people don't give, or give sparingly.

People don't give because of **fear.** They worry that if they give, then there will not be enough left over to meet their needs.

The sixth reason people don't give is because of **materialism.** Our culture has convinced us that we always need the best and the latest thing on the market. The advertiser's job is to make us discontent with what we have so that we will buy what they have.

The seventh reason people don't give because of **selfishness.** We all have to fight the urge to put ourselves first. Selfishness tempts us to hold on to what we have, whether it is our time, talents, or money. It's mine, mine, mine!

The final reason people don't give because of **a lack of faith.** In God's economy, what goes around comes around. Or in Bible words, "Whatever a person sows, that they will reap." A lack of faith in God's promises holds us all back at some time or another.

Now have you noticed that one could teach on fear, materialism, selfishness, and faith, and say nothing about tithing? These four examples apply to many areas of our lives but are particularly applicable to tithing; they are some of the foundational reasons why teaching on tithing doesn't work.

Hey…I've just given you a great four-point sermon.

To summarize, pastors don't speak on tithing very often, and sometimes this is due to fear, i.e., fear that people will think, "All He want is my money." Also, our people tend to only hear about tithing or giving when the church is in trouble. Speaking on tithing might bring some change, but it is usually limited, minimal, and temporary. Preaching on tithing seldom deals with the underlying reasons why most people don't tithe.

Here are my recommendations.

We need to speak more about tithing and giving, rather than less. Preach on money regardless if the offerings are up or down. The more frequently we allow this subject to come up, the less awkward and uncomfortable it will seem when we talk about it. Schedule a few times a year to preach on this and take any opportunity you have when preaching your 'non-tithing' sermons to touch upon it if the sermon passage brings it (or something related to it) up. Remember, Jesus talked a lot about money, giving, materialism, and our attitudes about these things.

The next time you preach on tithing, be honest with your people about the reluctance you have to share on this topic. Tell them how pastors are afraid of turning people off, being misunderstood, etc.

Focus your tithing-sermons on the underlying reasons why people hold on to their money: fear, materialism, selfishness, and a lack of faith. Once again, topics Jesus regularly spoke on.

And don't forget to pray. Ask God to fill your church with generous people. Since we're mentioning prayer, if you are mad or irritated with your church, or even specific members of your church, due to a lack of giving, hold off until you have brought these feelings to God and received an adequate amount of healing so that your sermons can be filled with love and grace.

83

HOW TO HAVE A HOME RUN SERMON

Have you ever had a home run? I'm not referring to your glory days in high school. I mean a home run, out of the stadium, ball bouncing around in the parking lot, sermon. I've had a few, or at least I thought they were. And then again, there have been times when I thought I had a home "home run" only to hear from my wife later that afternoon, "You've done better." Ouch...foul!

One of the many things I enjoy about my job is being a preaching coach. Everyone, even the best of communicators, can become better, and the process of increasing one's effectiveness in speaking is greatly accelerated when one has an objective pair of ears to offer helpful suggestions. I want to share with you three essentials for a home-run sermon. When crafting your message always focus on Strong Content, Practical Application, and Dynamic Delivery.

Strong Content.

Here you are asking yourself if your teaching is biblically and theologically solid. Does the passage you are teaching from really say what you say it says? You need to know that what you're teaching is rock-solid because you've studied it out for yourself instead of merely passing something on that someone else has taught you. If you haven't had any training in the area of hermeneutics, I suggest you find a good book on the subject and read it.

Practical Application.

Every home-run sermon will answer the question, "So what?" Great sermons make great application for those who are listening. What are you giving them that they can take with them and apply during their week? And while I'm at it...make sure the application relates to their week, not yours. Most of your people live in a different world than you do. Scratch where they itch.

Dynamic Delivery.

Are you interesting to listen to, or boring? Do you have good eye contact, do you incorporate humor in your sermons, and do you have good fluctuation in your voice? Are you articulate? Are you dull or fascinating when preaching? Dave's rule #12: Bore your people, go to jail.

Don't settle for a single or a double. Your people deserve at least a triple and occasionally a home run. If you want to knock it into the stands, focus on Content, Application, and Delivery. Hum-now batter...sa-wing!

84

HOW TO DEVELOP AN EFFECTIVE SERMON INTRODUCTION

We've all been taught that a good sermon has an introduction, a body, and a conclusion. I'm a preaching coach, so I think a lot about these things. I've been speaking since I was a new Christian at the age of 16. That's a lot of speaking. Let me share with you some thoughts I have about sermon introductions.

1. Wait to develop your introduction until after you've completed the body of your sermon. Once you have a solid body, you will be in a better place to decide on the most fitting introduction. One reason why some sermons do not relate to the introduction ("Hey, I thought he said he was going to speak on _____, but instead

he's talking about _____.") is that the pastor began with crafting the introduction first.

2. Your introduction should accomplish three things: get my attention, make me want to listen to you, and tell me where we'll be going. People can tune out pretty fast. We don't have much time to capture them. A good sermon introduction does just that.

3. Introductions are short but sweet. Depending on how long your sermons usually are should help you decide how long your introductions should be. For example, if you preach fifteen to twenty minutes, your introduction should be about three minutes long. If you preach close to thirty minutes, your introduction can be up to five minutes. I just say this because some sermons I listen to take ten minutes or longer before the speaker gets into the body of their sermon. You don't have much time to get to the meat, so offer an appetizer and then serve the main course.

They say that visitors to your church will decide within seven minutes after getting out of their car whether or not they will be coming back. It's similar to sermons. You've got a few minutes to get their attention and make them want to listen to you. Work at developing a great introduction.

85

HOW TO HAVE A MORE POWERFUL AND EFFECTIVE SERMON

Along with coaching pastors and church leaders, I am a preaching coach. I love helping speakers become better speakers.

One of the most common problems I run into with speakers is that their sermon lacks focus.

To have a powerfully focused sermon, start with developing a powerfully focused outline. To do so, answer these three questions:

1. What is the Main Thing I want to say?
2. What are the main things I want to say about the Main Thing?

3. Are my main things sticking to the Main Thing? If you have too many main things, you will drift away from the Main Thing.

Keep repeating the Main Thing to your audience. It all starts with the Main Thing.

86

HOW TO CHOOSE A TOPIC TO PREACH ON

It's hard to come up with a sermon topic. Sometimes we pick topics that are of interest to us but might not be a topic our audience will find helpful. It takes time to pray and think and evaluate your current context in order to select a subject that will be timely. It's much easier to pick the first thing that pops into your mind and then convince yourself that it was the Spirit.

Here are some helpful questions to ask before or after you've chosen a topic:

1. "What can I bring to this audience or subject that is unique?" Now truth is truth, and I don't think we need to feel obligated to come up with something new every time we speak. However, you are a unique individual with a perspective

and life-experiences that are especially yours. What can you give your listeners? What can you give to the topic that will be unique?

2. "What do I think these people need to hear?" This takes time to determine. Ask your spouse. Ask your leaders what they think the congregation needs to hear. Ask members of your congregation what they think the need is. After you come up with a topic, try to be as objective as you can and ask...

3. "Why do I think they need to hear this?" Let's say you determine that the church needs to hear a sermon on 'love.' Why do you think that? "Well because of this...I'm going to speak on that." You may be misinterpreting the "this." The "this" could be a symptom of a greater need. Or...are you choosing the topic because one individual complained to you about something they think you need to speak on? Not good enough.

4. "What are the most important elements of this subject that I need to deal with?" Don't feel like you've got to say all that can be said on your particular topic. I've heard speakers say, "Well there's so much I could say about this I didn't know what to leave out." You'd better get good at knowing what to leave out, or your people will check out.

5. "If I had to reduce this message down to one sentence, what would it be?"

Determine the "it" and then let that be your guiding light. What do you want them to take home with them? Keep it simple, clear, obvious.

6. "Is it possible that there is a topic that could be more timely and appropriate?"

   One of your most effective tools for influence is your gift of teaching. Take the time to think through the topics you speak on. Use the questions I've suggested to help you pick topics that will be the right message at the right time for the right people.

7. And last, but certainly not least, because of prayer and waiting upon God, did you have any sense of what He wants you to preach on? Go here first and then you can start with question #1.

87

HOW TO LIVE WITHOUT COMMENTARIES

Some years ago I did something I never dreamed possible. I donated all of my commentaries and bible study helps to my alma mater. There were a few old or rare volumes that I kept for sentimental reasons or in hopes of impressing someone in the future who might see my library, but other than that, I boxed them up and dropped them off. I must admit, as I walked away I had mixed feelings. I felt like a parent abandoning their child on someone's doorstep.

There were two reasons why I gave away a big portion of my library. First, online bible study helps were becoming so abundant that I hardly needed to open 'real' books anymore. And second, I discovered that I so seldom needed to turn to commentaries to put together a good sermon that they didn't justify the space they were taking up on my bookshelves. On those rare occasions that I needed to look something up, I could do so online.

Here are some random thoughts I have about commentaries and the place they play in sermon preparation.

If you spend more than an hour a week reading commentaries, you're probably spending too much time reading commentaries.

If you already have a Bachelors or Masters in Bible & Theology, or something similar, you've probably been exposed to an adequate amount of bible and theology classes. Hours of commentary reading will probably not result in you discovering anything new, i.e., 'new' from a scholarly, commentary, academic point of view. If you do learn something new (and there's always something new) the practicality of it will probably not be so great as to justify the time spent.

Assuming that you have some formal training in Bible and Theology, the only time you might want to turn to a commentary is if you are dealing with a controversial or difficult passage and you feel a need for some other opinions on the passage.

If you have no formal training in Bible and Theology, then go to the local Christian bookstore and find a few commentaries designed for laymen. These volumes are easier to understand, typically make the application for you, contain all the important stuff, and are less expensive than the larger, more scholarly commentaries.

When you need input from commentaries, take advantage of the free tools online, you'll save time and money.

Discover which website is good for what. For example, one site might be good for commentaries and another good for a concordance. One might be strong if you're looking for a parallel bible while another one excels in Greek and Hebrew. One might have a better selection of word study helps or Bible dictionaries than another. Once you've discovered the strengths of each website create a link to each one, change their names to reflect what you'll use them for, i.e., commentaries, bible dictionaries, Greek, etc., and put them all in a folder on your desktop. And there you have it, your own custom library.

PEOPLE PROBLEMS

88

HOW TO DEAL WITH GOSSIP

I'm into my eleventh year of coaching pastors. That's a long time to be listening to, encouraging, and resourcing pastors and church leaders. But I'm telling you, if I had twenty bucks for every time I've spoken to a pastor who is dealing with someone in their church that is a gossip, I'd be a rich man. Well, maybe not rich, but I would have a significant amount of discretionary fun-money in my wallet. My point is, if you have a church, you will have gossip. Everybody has to deal with it at some time. You might be dealing with it right now. Gossip (and it's cousin Slander) are two of the most dangerous sicknesses to infect a church.

Let me share with you seven steps to deal with gossip in your church.

1. Compile a list of all the verses in the Bible where the words 'gossip' and 'slander' appear.

2. Come up with a working definition of gossip and slander.
3. Review the verses on your list and the definitions you came up with. Using a scale of one to ten (one being lowest) score the degree of problem you have in your church or with a specific individual.
4. Clearly identify the guilty party(s).
5. If you were to confront this person, what response might you expect from them?
6. What risks are you taking by confronting them and what risks are you taking by not confronting them?
7. Are you willing to get bloody over this? You probably will. Gossips and Slanderers usually don't repent, stop, or leave the church without putting up a fight. If the one doing the gossip has a great deal of influence in the church, you could get in trouble at best, and lose your job at worst.

You might be surprised to hear me say this, but my experience in working with pastors is that they fail to deal with gossip early on, and this results in the problem growing and growing until they have a much more serious situation on their hands than when gossip originally raised its ugly head.

If you decide to confront the person don't forget to:

1. Pray before you go.
2. Take someone with you.
3. Don't sugarcoat the seriousness of the situation to the person.
4. Don't be afraid to tell the person to stop it or they will have to leave.
5. Don't forget to duck.

89

HOW TO DEAL WITH SOMEONE WHO IS CAUSING YOU GRIEF

I f I saw you as God sees you, what would I see? If you saw me as God sees me, what would you see? If you saw that person in your church that is causing you grief as God sees them, what would you see?

Is there someone in your church that is hurting you, resisting your leadership, opposing you, saying bad things about you? If not presently, certainly there has been such a person in your past, and there will certainly be one in your future. One of the frustrating things about Jesus is that he asks us to do the seemingly impossible. Want an example? How about, "Love your enemies and pray for those who persecute you."

It's hard to lead without love. It's hard to love someone who is acting in an unlovable way towards you, your spouse, your family, or your church. How then can practice what Christ asked of us? Where can we start?

I'm not going to pretend that this will be easy, but if we can see that person as God sees them, we will (or God will) have something to build upon. Ask yourself, "If I saw _____ as God sees him, how would I see him?" Ask God, "Father, how do you see _____?"

What do you see, what do you hear the Father saying to you?

God is love. God loves that person who is causing trouble for you. This does not justify their behavior or minimize how they are making you feel, but it is a Divine perspective that we can forget, and one we will need to remember if we are going to move towards love, rather than away from love. Seeing people as God sees them is the first step towards love.

Are you willing to take that first step? There will be other steps you might need to take before you're ready to confront and correct that person, but don't worry about those steps yet. Just take the first step.

90

HOW TO RECOGNIZE AND RESPOND TO A DYSFUNCTIONAL CHURCH BOARD

M any Pastors face the challenge of working with a dysfunctional board.

"Not me. I've got an awesome church board."

I believe you. I'm happy for you. I certainly don't want to give the impression that all church boards are dysfunctional. I'm working with, and have worked with many pastors who have incredible leadership teams and church boards. However, I know enough pastors who have, in my opinion, a dysfunctional board.

Once when recording a podcast for 200churches. com on this subject, I was asked, "What do you mean by "dysfunctional board?" That's a good question.

A dysfunctional board is one that sees their job as 'business-focused' rather than 'spiritual.'

A dysfunctional board is one that fights and opposes every idea the pastor has.

A dysfunctional board is one that ties the hands of the pastor, thus preventing the pastor from leading the church.

A dysfunctional board is one that is filled with spiritually immature board members.

A dysfunctional board is one that is unclear as to what their job is.

A dysfunctional board is one that thinks they know what their job is, but they don't.

A dysfunctional board is one that has members that should have stepped down a long time ago.

If a pastor is afraid of or intimidated by any board member, there's a good chance he or she has a dysfunctional church board.

Unfortunately, many congregations have established policies that can easily contribute to a dysfunctional church board. For example: In many churches, board members are voted in by the congregation and often the congregation has no idea of the type of person who is qualified to serve on a church board. In many churches, the board's job is to handle the 'business-part' of the church with little or no concept of their position being a spiritual calling requiring spiritual and godly leaders. In many churches there are no term-limits, so dysfunctional board members serve until they resign or die. In many churches, the board has too much power and authority over the pastor. These are just a few examples of church polity that the pastor can have very little power to change.

So what's a pastor to do if they find themselves in a situation like this? Here are four suggestions.

1. Pray.

    Ask the Father to change the hearts of your board. You could ask that the Father to remove the dysfunctional board member (I'm not talking about lightning) so you don't have to. Maybe God needs to change some dysfunction in you that is contributing to the dysfunction in the board.

2. Gear up for the long haul.

    Be patient. Leading a board from dysfunctional to functional is not going to happen overnight. This is going to take time. Sometimes it will seem like two steps forward and one step back, sometimes two steps back.

3. Invest relationally with the board members you find difficult to work with. Often the resistance we experience from dysfunctional board members is the result of a lack of trusting relationships. Try to spend time together, not to discuss church stuff, but to have fun and get to know each other better.

4. Re-educate your team as to what the role of a board should be. Again, this will take time.

91

HOW TO AVOID NUMBSKULLS

So it's after church on Sunday. You've preached your heart out. You've been at the building since 8:00 am. The last chair has been put away. Your stomach is growling and you're tired. Just as you reach to turn off the lights, Brother Bill comes up to you and wants to know your position on women in the ministry. Since Bill considers himself somewhat of a self-taught theologian, you know he will not be satisfied with a one or two sentence answer. You say, "You insensitive, arrogant numbskull, can't you see I'm trying to get out of here?"

Well...you'd probably never say that...but you'd like to.

Position-papers can save a lot of time and let you address the individual's question in a thorough way without taking the time right there and then. When I was pastoring, I had position papers on a wide range of controversial subjects. Some examples:

> Women in The Ministry
> The Gifts of The Holy Spirit
> The Role of The Elder
> Church Government, i.e., how we make
> decisions here at the church
> Tithing, etc.

I developed the content of these papers based on past messages I'd delivered. I honed my teaching notes down to the bare essentials and created an 8.5 X 11 double-sided tri-fold brochure, printed off copies and made them available each Sunday morning at our literature table. Eventually, the same documents appeared on our website.

It was great to be able to refer someone to one of my papers. That way, when someone wanted information that I did not have time to give, or if a controversial subject was brought up in a large group setting, I could tell them to visit our table or website.

The bottom line is that it's always better to hand someone a brochure than to call them a numbskull.

92

HOW TO DEAL WITH
BULLIES IN THE CHURCH

In Junior High I was one of those skinny kids (you'd never believe it if you saw me now) who wasn't into sports, was self-conscious, and lived in fear of being beaten up by a bully. I was very aware of who the bullies were and where they hung out. My life-preserving strategy was simple, avoid the bullies, and you won't get beaten up. Apparently it worked because I made it through Junior High without ever getting pounded.

Pastor Jim (not his real name) had a problem on his hands, and he wanted to process it with me during one of our coaching calls. Bubba (not his real name but I thought that was a good name for a bully) had been a church board member, had taken a year off according to the church by-laws, and now was letting everyone know that when his break was over he intended

to return to his position on the board, pending nomi-
nation and approval by the congregation.

> "So what's the problem?" I asked.
> "None of my current board members
> want him back."
> "Why?"
> "He's really difficult to work with. Bubba
> is a big guy, boisterous, and he uses his
> size and words to intimidate others.
> People in the church are uncomfort-
> able around him, and some have even
> shared that they are afraid of him. But
> he's been in the church for a long time,
> and he has a lot of influence, even if it's
> bad influence.
> "Sounds like you have a bully on your
> hands."
> "I think you're right."

Church bullies come in all shapes and sizes. They
might not look exactly like Bubba, but they are just as
much a bully. Church bullies intimidate and threat-
en, overtly or covertly, consciously or unconsciously.
They might use their influence or money or ministry
position to pressure you and others to do what they
want. Some have been known to actually threaten the
pastor.

"We voted you in and we can vote you out. I was here before you came and I will be here after you're gone."

The only way to deal with a bully is to walk right up to them and smack them good and hard in the nose.

No...not really, I'm kidding...kind of.

Church bullies won't stop until someone stops them. You get what you tolerate. Do you have a church bully who needs to hear, "STOP IT"?

Confronting a bully is scary and risky. It can be dangerous, but not as dangerous as letting the bully continue to bully. It's not uncommon for me to find a pastor who is intimidated by one or two people in their church and those one or two make life miserable for the pastor and can put a damper on the over all ministry of the church.

Do you have a bully on your hands? If so, might I suggest a few steps, none of which involves slugging them in the nose?

1. Devote some time in prayer to make sure that you are really dealing with a bully and not something else. If timing isn't everything, it's close enough. Is the Father releasing you to confront the person now or later?

2. Find a couple wise, mature, trusted people in your church who have the same concerns about this person that you have, who will accompany you to a meeting with this person.

3. Send a well crafted letter to this person stating that you and a couple of others would like to meet with them to discuss some concerns you have about their behavior. I like the 'letter first' approach because it gives the person some time to think about things and because nobody likes being surprised.

4. At the meeting get right to the point. Don't bother buttering them up and then dropping the bomb. Give specific examples of the behavior that is unacceptable and why it's unacceptable. Communicate to them that you are for them and would love to meet with them on a regular basis to help them grow in these areas. But be firm and clear that their behavior will no longer be tolerated.

This is scary. This is risky. They might blow out of the church and take their money and their friends with them. They might lead a campaign to get you fired. You might get fired. But there are many churches across this nation of ours that are being influenced by bullies rather than godly, humble leaders.

Someone, sometime, has to stand up to them face to face and say, "STOP IT!"

93

HOW TO KNOW WHEN IT'S TIME TO SUGGEST THAT SOMEONE LEAVE YOUR CHURCH

I can remember fishing with my grandpa when I was a little boy. Fred Flowerday, one of nine boys and a girl born to a farmer in Nebraska. Fred knew how to fish. Grandpa taught me about 'keepers.' Those of you who fish know that 'keepers' are fish worthy of... well, keeping. If the fish was too small or looked sickly, Grandpa would say, "Throw it back." All others were keepers.

Now if we apply this metaphor to newcomers at your church it's easy to sound callous and disinterested. But the fact is that some people will be right for your church, and some won't. Some will be keepers, and some should be released to go swimming in another pond. It won't do you any good, in the long run, to encourage someone to stay and get involved in your church, if you know the church will not be a right fit for them. Save yourself, and your new fish, a headache. Be comfortable in saying, "I don't think this church is a good fit for you." You're not being mean (provided you speak caringly); you're being a good leader. You're being good to them and good to your church.

If you sense that your new catch has a different agenda than yours…let them go. If your fish is pushing for a different style of worship than you want…let them go. If they want you to be more charismatic than you are, or less charismatic than you are, if they want you to be something other than what you are, they will be frustrated with you, and eventually, you will be frustrated with them. Express to them that it's okay for them to leave, no hard feelings…let them go.

Now I understand that you want to grow your church. You don't want people to leave; you want them to stay. I've been there. I know what it's like to feel you've got a 'keeper' because they seem so excited about the Lord, so talented, so experienced, and they believe in tithing. Sure you might have some reservations, but hey…they tithe.

All people have worth, but not all are worth the energy of trying to keep them happy when your church is simply not right for them. It's not going to be worth it for you to try and fit a square peg in a round hole. You will either damage the square peg or damage the round hole to make them fit. Either way, you've got damage.

Maybe you've been struggling with someone in your church for a long time. They always seem to be kicking against the goads. Maybe your church is not a good fit for them. Have enough integrity and courage to suggest they try someplace else. Be kind, choose your words carefully, and then show them the door. You barely have enough energy to care for those who are a good fit for your church, let alone those who aren't a good fit. Keep the keepers and be willing to stock someone else's pond. Who knows, maybe at another church they will be happy and flourish because they've found a church better suited for them?

94

HOW TO KNOW IF IT'S TIME TO FIGHT, OR TIME TO STAY OUT OF THE RING

I nside the ring it's a sport, outside the ring it's a crime. You guessed it; I'm referring to professional boxing. I'll return to the absurdity of this sport and how it relates to leadership in a moment, but, if you want a good laugh, google "boxing quotes" and enjoy yourself. Here are a few I came across:

Bob Hope: "I was called "Rembrandt" Hope in my boxing days because I spent so much time on the canvas."

Randall "Tex" Cobb: "When I got up I stuck to my plan — stumbling forward and getting hit in the face."

Max Baer, when asked for his definition of fear: "Standing across the ring from Joe Louis and knowing he wants to go home early."

Muhammad Ali: "It's just a job. Grass grows, birds fly, waves pound the sand. I beat people up."

I think it's this last quote from Ali that sums up how ridiculous boxing seems to me…we've sanctioned a job, the purpose of which is to beat someone up. But what does this have to do with leadership?

Be selective with who or what you're willing to climb into the ring for. Choose your fights wisely.

A college professor of mine once said, "Some things are worth fighting for, and some things are worth dying for. And most things aren't worth either." Sometimes leaders can make issues of things that aren't that important. We need to ask ourselves, "Is this something I need to get in the ring over?"

Are you in the ring with someone? Is it worth it? Could someone else get in the ring in your place? Will letting the issue go be all that bad? Never underestimate your ability to think something is really important when it's not.

In the past I've made issues of things that, looking back, I can now see weren't as important as I thought they were. There have been things I thought were problems that were not, and my thinking they were, ended up making them a problem, a different problem, a bigger problem.

When in doubt get advice from someone objective and disassociated from the situation. Don't get in the ring unless you really need to.

VOLUNTEERS & LEADERSHIP DEVELOPMENT

95

HOW TO HELP YOUR VOLUNTEERS QUIT

Like it or not, the church is a volunteer-driven organization. Unless, of course, your church is so small that you are the volunteer. That's pretty small. In fact, the smaller your church is, the less you need leaders and the more you need helpers or, volunteers. Now apparently some of you are pretty good at losing volunteers. I say this because so many pastors want to talk to me about how frustrated they are with their dysfunctional and dwindling volunteer base. There's always room for improvement. I want to share with you how you can become more effective in helping your volunteers quit.

First of all, over commit the few volunteers that you have. Volunteers love this. If they are good at doing one task, they will probably be good at two, or three, or four.

Keep them in the dark as to what exactly it is you want them to do. For example, if you want them to do A, B, C and D, only tell them about A and C. It's best to spring things on them after they've signed on the dotted line. But don't have them sign anything. Whatever you do, don't give them a job description (wait, you'd better call it a 'ministry-description' or you'll be accused of running the church like a business.) The bottom line is, don't put your expectations down on paper. This way you can add things to their job without them knowing which will give you the freedom to be irritated at them for not doing what you never told them to do.

Whenever you meet with them, limit the conversation to how they and their ministry are doing. Don't check in about their family, their marriage, and their soul. You only have so much time, focus on the important things, i.e., how they are helping you grow the church. Volunteers love this.

When you do meet with them, make sure to list off what needs improvement, Volunteers love this. And whatever you do, never let them tell you what they think needs improvement in your areas of responsibility. Hey...who died and made them the boss?

Don't bother praising them for a job well done in front of others. You don't want this to go to their heads; after all, they should be looking for praise from God, not man. Don't feed that thing.

Make sure that their commitment is until Christ returns. Jesus didn't take a break. You don't get a break. Why should they expect one? Believe me, volunteers love open-ended commitments.

Training? Who needs training? You're an intuitive leader, they should be an intuitive volunteer. And don't go quoting Eph. 4:11,12 to me. That was easy for Paul to say because he never had a busy schedule like yours.

And finally...always, always, always expect your volunteers to be as committed to the church as you are. You don't have a life outside of the church, why should they? And if they dare to admit that they don't have enough time to volunteer any more than they already are, you can always resort to guilt and shame. Guilt and shame are very effective motivators. In fact, you should plan to regularly preach on how screwed up Christian's priorities are. Volunteers love this.

I hope you've found this helpful. Now go out there and lose some volunteers. God be with you.

96

HOW TO KEEP YOUR BEST PEOPLE

In our last church, I had possibly the best children's ministry director in my twenty-eight years of pastoring. Carrie was one of those gifted people who had a passion for kids, was pro-active, and you never had to worry about her. But one day she came into my office and said, "Dave, sometimes I feel like the only reason we meet is to talk about my ministry. I don't feel like you care about me as a person, I'm just someone that helps you accomplish your vision for the church."

Ouch!

You know what? She was right. Of course I cared about Carrie, but is was true, our one-on-one meetings were all about how her department was doing. I never met with Carrie to simply talk about life, how was she doing, etc. I apologized. She accepted my apology, and we were able to move forward. But Carrie helped me learn a life-long lesson.

Your leaders need two types of meetings.

Leadership Team meetings. Even if you only have a few leaders, you need to gather them for prayer, communication, vision-casting, and leadership development. But never forget, group meetings accomplish something different than the one-on-one meetings. Understanding this difference is essential if you want to keep your best leaders.

One-on-one meetings. You need time to check in with your leaders and find out how they are doing, not just how their ministry is doing. Ask questions like:

How's your relationship with Jesus?

If you had to choose one word to describe your current relationship with Jesus, what would it be?

If they are married: If you had one word to describe your current relationship with your spouse, your children, etc., what would it be?

How can I better serve you?

I guess you could talk about their ministry in a 'one-on-one,' but make sure you start out with the personal stuff first. And if your whole time with them ends up being about personal stuff, that's okay. Follow-up sometime later to find out how their ministry is doing.

Ellen once reminded me, "Dave, it's all about people, not programs. People before programs." I've never forgotten that.

Make sure that group meetings and one-on-one meetings show up in your calendar. If you want to keep your best people, give time to your best people. Show them you care about them, not just care about how they are serving in the church.

97

HOW TO DISCERN IF YOU NEED LEADERS OR HELPERS

I think it was John Maxwell that said, "Everything rises or falls on leadership." The group I was a part of (The Vineyard), drilled into us the need to 'raise up leaders.' Some experts have even told pastors that your church will only grow as large as your base of leaders. I'm not sure that's always true, but it might be close enough.

Often pastors want to talk to me about leadership development. And if they don't bring up the subject, eventually I will ask them, "What are you doing to raise up new leaders?" But first I want to know how many active adults (adults, not adults and children) they have in their church, why? Because...

The smaller the church, the less the pastor needs leaders and the more the pastor needs helpers.

Now let there be no mistake about it, leaders will come from your team of helpers. Of those who are helping you, someone will stand out and catch your attention. Chances are, this could be a future leader.

The smaller your church, the more likely it will be that you have more, sometimes way more, helpers than you have leaders. You see, if you are searching for leaders, you are probably looking for a degree of maturity and commitment to Jesus and the church. You may, or may not have such a person. But if you are looking for helpers, the bar is a little lower, and you will have more to choose from. Besides, it's better to wait until you have the right kind of person to call a leader, than it is to put someone in leadership prematurely and later regret it.

Once you call someone a 'leader' everything changes. Calling someone a leader changes their relationship with you and your relationship with them. Calling someone a leader changes the way your church thinks of the person. And, sorry to say this, sometimes people change, and not always for the better, once you start calling them a leader. For example, they might think this (calling them a leader) means more than you intended it to mean. I suggest that you hold off calling anyone a leader until you've had enough time to know if they are 'leading' in the way you want a leader to lead.

Do you need leaders or do you only need helpers?
Here are some steps you might find helpful:

1. If you think you need a leader, what is it specifically that they need to lead?
2. What concrete reasons do you have for thinking they would be a good leader of (fill in the blank)?
3. Do you need to call them a leader or could you call them something else?

Who are your helpers?

1. Who among your helpers stands out the most?
2. Who among your helpers comes in at second place?
3. Pray over these people and ask the Father to show you if he regards them as potential leaders.
4. Begin to pour your time into them.
5. At some point, but only if you think you have a future leader on your hands, let them know that you think they have potential.

Almost all leaders started out as helpers. Know who your helpers are, and you will eventually know who some of your future leaders will be.

98

HOW TO GIVE YOUR LEADERS WHAT THEY REALLY NEED

A pastor needs to know not only how to recruit, train, and release leaders...they also need to know how to maintain leaders. If you don't maintain your leaders they might not remain your leaders.

Here are six things leaders need from their pastor. Read over the list and ask yourself how you're doing in giving your leaders what they need.

1. Leaders need our time and attention.
2. Leaders need tools and resources specific to their area of ministry.
3. Leaders need someone to hold them accountable for their spiritual growth.
4. Leaders need someone they can look up to, i.e., an example to follow.

5. Leaders want to feel that we care about them, and not just the role they play in the church.
6. Leaders want to feel that they are included in the decision-making process.

How's your maintenance?

99

HOW TO PAY YOUR VOLUNTEERS

One day, during our second church plant, I was sitting across the table from a successful land-developer, and we were talking about the similarities of starting a business and starting a church. I suggested that they are very much the same, but my friend pointed out what he felt was a major difference.

> "I think it's much harder for you to run a church than it is for me to run a company."
> "How so?" I asked.
> "In my company I can motivate with money or with losing your job. In your business, you work with volunteers. It's much harder to work with volunteers than real employees."

He was right.

If you are pastoring a smaller church, chances are (unless you are bi-vocational) there is no one other than you on the church payroll. You do not pay your workforce. They are volunteers. However, just because they volunteer does not mean that they do not need to be paid. There are many ways to pay your volunteers other than money. Here are some suggestions:

1. Mention their name on Sunday mornings during your sermon to commend them for a job well done.

2. Spend time with them. Take them out for lunch or coffee.

3. Give them little gifts like a Starbucks card or something similar.

4. Pray for them and let them know you are praying for them.

5. Have a ministry appreciation night where, for example, you get all the workers together from your Children's Ministry for a dinner that you provide. Pamper them, make them feel special. This doesn't have to be costly, but it does need to be nice.

6. Give out awards on Sunday mornings for volunteers who have done a good job or recently completed a new assignment.

The biggest difference between a pastor and a manager of a secular business is that the pastor works almost exclusively with people that are not paid. The smart leader will learn how to pay his or her volunteers.

100

HOW TO IDENTIFY AND FISH YOUR VOLUNTEER PONDS

It seems like you can never have enough volunteers. And often, because of this, the pastor finds him or herself filling in the gaps, which means, doing things they should not have to do, instead of the things they should be doing. This then, brings us to the subject of 'delegation.'

Whether you're searching for more volunteers to help in the various ministries of your church, or looking for someone to delegate responsibilities that are currently on your shoulders, here are my "Ones, Twos and Threes of Delegation" that will help you identify potential volunteers.

First, get out your church phone directory, or whatever list you keep that tells you the adults that are currently involved in your church. Count someone as an "adult" beginning at the age of sixteen.

Look over your list of those people that are already adequately involved in the church. These are the types that are doing their part, and therefore, you would be reluctant to ask them to take on any more responsibility. Write a number one next to their name.

Next, look over your list of those people that are currently doing nothing in your church. Every church has these types. You know what I mean. Basically, they just show up once in a while on Sunday mornings, maybe if you're lucky they drop a dollar in the offering and that's about it. Write a number three next to their name.

Finally, look over your list of those people that are somewhere between the ones and the threes. These are people that are contributing, or involved in some small way, but the commitment is so little that they could easily take on more without becoming overly committed. For example, you are grateful for the person who stands at the door and hands out the bulletins, but if that is all that they do, they could maybe do more. You appreciate those who pass the offering plates or baskets, but that is not a very high commitment or time-consuming ministry. Write a number two next to their name.

Think of your twos and your threes as "volunteer ponds" that you can fish in. Over time some of your twos will move up to become ones. Over time some of your threes will move up to become twos. On the other hand, some twos and threes will never rise above their current status. But you never know, miracles do happen.

If you have a significant area of ministry that you want to delegate, you don't want to give it to a two or a three. Important areas of ministry need to be delegated to a one. But if your ones are already adequately committed, you will need to take some responsibilities off of their plates and onto the plates of your twos or your threes, and therefore, free up your ones so they can take on what you need to delegate.

My 'Ones, Twos, and Threes of Delegation' will help you identify who you have to work with when seeking volunteers. There are no guarantees. They may still say no, but at least this is a step in the right direction and one that should help

spread ministry responsibilities out to a broader base of your congregation.

ABOUT THE AUTHOR

Dave Jacobs was a pastor for twenty-eight years before retiring in 2006 and founding Small Church Pastor, an organization that provides encouragement, coaching, consulting, and resources for pastors and leaders of churches of all sizes, but with a focus on smaller churches. Dave and Ellen have been married for thirty-eight years. They have five adult children, eleven grandchildren, and love living in beautiful Medford, Oregon. Dave is the author of 'Mile Wide, Inch Deep: Experiencing God Beyond the Shallows, Soul Care for Busy Pastors and the Rest of Us,' and 'Belligerent Believers.'

> You can reach Dave at:
> dave@smallchurchpastor.com
> and find Dave at:
> www.smallchurchpastor.com
> www.davejacobs.net
> and Twitter @thinkmonk

Made in the USA
Middletown, DE
27 April 2020

92117926R00176